MW00790775

JESUS & LAO TZU

Adventures with the Tao Te Ching

Jesus & Lao Tzu

Adventures with the Tao Te Ching

George Breed

Anamchara Books

Copyright © 2014 by Anamchara Books, a division of Harding House Publishing Service, Inc. All rights reserved. No part of this publication may be reproduced or transmitted in any form or by any means, electronic or mechanical, including photocopying, recording, taping, or any information storage and retrieval system, without permission from the publisher.

Anamchara Books
Vestal, NY 13850
www.anamcharabooks.com

Printed in the United States of America.

9 8 7 6 5 4 3 2

Paperback ISBN: 978-1-62524-107-8
ebook ISBN: 978-1-62524-108-5
Library of Congress Control Number: 2014934094

The chapters of the Tao Te Ching presented here are the publisher's own version, based on the 1891 translation by J. Legge.

INTRODUCTION

For the past several decades, I have studied the teachings of Jesus in both the canonical and apocryphal gospels. During that same time period, I also tracked down as many English translations of the Tao Te Ching as I could find; in the process, I became quite familiar with the consciousness of Lao Tzu, the reputed author. I came to feel that I knew both Jesus and Lao Tzu personally. When someone else's consciousness becomes your consciousness, this is as personal as it gets. I wanted to write about the experience.

Other books have been written of course, pointing out the parallels between Jesus and Lao Tzu. (I recommend *Christ: The Eternal Tao* and *Jesus and Lao Tzu: The Parallel Sayings*.) What I felt I had to offer, however, was the triad that came into being as I interacted with the Tao Te Ching: the consciousness state of Jesus as implied by his sayings (Christ consciousness), the consciousness state of Lao Tzu as implied by his sayings (Tao consciousness), and my own consciousness state. My role in this triad was to introduce Jesus and Lao Tzu to each other within my own being. We merged while remaining distinct.

As I pondered how to express this in writing, something wonderful happened. Jesus and Lao Tzu appeared in my writing room most every morning over a period of several months. They were quite comfortable with each other, relaxed and friendly. The three of us wandered the streets and countryside of Flagstaff, Arizona (where I live), and we had various adventures and conversations in which they educated me further on the meaning of a particular Tao Te Ching chapter.

The force of their personalities made me feel like Carlos Castaneda must have felt in his adventures with Don Juan. I was definitely the student, and they were the teachers. Once, they came in and rousted me out of bed, flinging the bed covers aside and leaving me there in wonderment. I always felt comfortable and safe with them, though, and I knew that their antics were their method of teaching. They were cracking the hard nut of my consciousness and opening me to deeper understandings.

In this book, in most cases, each adventure we had is prefaced by a rendition of the particular Tao Te Ching chapter relevant to that day's adventure. I use "Jesus" and "Christ" interchangeably, knowing that Jesus is the human manifestation of Christ and that Christ is the spiritual essence of Jesus. I regard the two as one. Lao Tzu can be roughly translated as "The Old Dude," and *Tao* is usually translated as "Way," *Te* as "Virtue," and *Ching* as "Book": hence, "The Book of the Way and Its Virtue." Jesus said "I am the Way, the Truth, and the Life." In Lao Tzu's language, Jesus is saying he is the Tao and Its Virtue. Lao Tzu did not say he was the Tao, but he did say It was birthing him.

Though Lao Tzu says no name can name it, he calls the Source from which all is continually arising the Tao or Way. Jesus calls the Source the Father. He says that he and the Father are one. So are we all. But the difference between Jesus and us is that Jesus knew he was one with the Father—and we generally don't. We think of ourselves as separate from the Source, the Father, the Tao, the Way. By considering ourselves as separate, we *are* separate.

We have named ourselves, we have named and are naming everything. The very process of naming sets us apart from the rest of the living reality. We put our egg of consciousness on the wall we create between ourselves and our Source. What a setup! No surprise that the egg falls and splatters into a zillion pieces. No forces in the named world can put it back together again.

Jesus says that he is the Way. He is the Way waying, the Tao taoing, the Source sourcing. He invites us to do the same, to open our consciousness as the Source sourcing. As we shall see, Lao Tzu issues a similar invitation.

Jesus, Lao Tzu, and I sit here together. They have twinkles in their eyes and merry hearts. They laugh at my desire to comment on their words. They do not comment on my words, they remind me—so how can I have such presumption?

"Because you are a sump pump," says Lao Tzu. We all three chortle at his wordplay. "You wish to pump in wisdom from beyond."

"The wisdom is here and walks among us, if we but have eyes to see and ears to hear," says Jesus.

I already love these two. What greater friends could I ever hope to have?

They look at me and smile.

We shall see what unfolds.

1A
the wheel we need to be

The Way that can be stepped on

is not the enduring and unchanging Way.

The name that can be named

is not the enduring and unchanging name.

When we think of it as having no name,

it is the Source of heaven and earth;

when we think of it as having a name,

it is still the Mother of all things.

Jesus leaned forward and said, "My buddy, Lao Tzu here, is always talking about the Way. I also spoke of the Way—and it got me into a lot of trouble. I said that I am the Way, the Truth, and the Life. No one comes to the Father but by me. Holy Moses! Has that been misunderstood! Let's get democratic here.

My aim is for each person to be able to say those words with deep understanding."

Lao Tzu nodded. "Yes, Jesus! When we know we are the Way waying, we live in a different world. Our consciousness has changed, as Georgie Boy here would say."

I laughed, grateful to be included in the conversation. "I love you too, Old Dude."

"I'm glad you two are having a love feast," Jesus said, "but I have more to say. People set up a religion around me and that's okay. In the physical world, the forming always needs a form. The danger is that the form assumes priority, and that the forming hardens into set opinion."

Lao Tzu nodded again. "Well said. I put it this way. 'Thirty spokes converge on a hub, but it's the emptiness that makes a wheel work.'"

Jesus clapped his hands and jumped to his feet. "Yes! Don't get hung up on the wheel! The wheel will continue revolving and evolving. It's the boundless openness of our Father that we must allow to embody us. Then each of us will be the wheel we need to be."

1B
beginnings

Without desire, we find the deep Mystery;

With desire, we touch only its outer fringes.

Within these two perspectives, the Mystery is really the same;

but as development takes place,

it receives different names.

"Lao Tzu," said Jesus as we walked through an open meadow, "this reminds me of my reply to some of my students when they were so desirous of knowing the end of things."

Lao Tzu looked at him and raised an eyebrow.

Jesus answered his silent question. "I told them the place of the beginning is the place of the end."

Lao Tzu chuckled. "I bet they really understood that!"

Jesus gave his beard a thoughtful tug. "Well, a few were starting to. They were accustomed to living according to the 'outer fringes' and not according to the 'deep Mystery,' as you put it. They did not know that their outer perceptions are determined by their inner essence, that their perceptions of the world are determined by the quality and capaciousness of their inner being."

Lao Tzu shrugged. He seemed a little uncomfortable with Jesus' amplification of his words. "So I gather you did not go into long philosophical discussions about this."

Jesus laughed. "No. I responded with a question: 'Have you found the beginning so that you now seek the end?'"

Lao Tzu doubled over with laughter. "Lord, Jesus! You are as bad as I am!"

"Well, I added a little more to it. I told them: 'Blessed is anyone who will stand up in the beginning and thereby know the end and never die.'"

By this time, we had climbed out of the meadow, and now we were sitting atop a large rock, looking out across the valley below. We sat without speaking for a while, and then Lao Tzu broke the silence. "That's true about never dying. When you know the beginning and the end, you know the source from which they flow."

1c

my eyes were spinning

Together we call them the Mystery.
Where the Mystery is the deepest
is the gate of all that is subtle and wonderful.

When I asked Jesus and Lao Tzu to explain this to me, Lao Tzu sighed. "Go ahead, Jesus, I am tired of talking. The talk that can be talked is not the Talk." He leaned back on the rock and closed his eyes.

Jesus smiled. "George, can you see your eyes?"

I shook my head. "Only by looking in a mirror. But that is not really seeing my eyes, only their reflection. No, I cannot see my eyes."

"So what is seeing through your eyes, those eyes you cannot see?"

I shrugged. "Some of our scientists say it is a piece of meat we call the brain."

"And what is producing this piece of meat?"

I shrugged again. "I do not know. I can put names on it: Chance, God, Allah, the Godhead, Tao."

Lao Tzu squirmed a little on the rock beside me. "We have already been through that." Clearly, he couldn't keep himself from jumping in with his two cents, because he added, "Those names are not It. The name that can be named is not the eternal name."

"Exactly!" said Jesus. He turned back to me. "Think of yourself as looking out to infinity and eventually you see the back of your own head. Enter there and look out to infinity. Who is looking through your eyes?"

"Infinity?" I ventured.

"Yes. And what is infinity?"

"I do not know."

"Exactly," said Jesus. " This is the Mystery. This is the dark beyond dark. This is the Door to all beginnings."

Lao Tzu burst out laughing. "Look at the poor boy, Jesus! His eyes are spinning. I think he has gone out of his mind."

"Good!" said Jesus.

2A
dissolving the fragments

Everyone in the world knows the beauty of the beautiful,

and by knowing this, everyone has an idea about what ugliness is;

everyone knows what skill looks like—

and so they also know what the lack of skill is.

Lao Tzu gave me a smile. He could see the consternation in my heart.

"But Lao Tzu," I protested, "you are saying that by thinking of beauty, I call ugliness into the world! I cannot accept that!"

He burst out laughing. "And *now* you are calling into the world what you can accept and what you can't. You're a living example of what I am saying."

I turned to Jesus, hoping for some help, but he threw his hands up in the air. "Don't look at me! All humans are judgmental, dividing the world into this and that. This you love and cherish. That you fear and disdain. You love and cherish everything that you perceive to be in favor of your sweet ass. Some of you love me to save your ass. And some of you *won't* love me to save your ass!"

Lao Tzu and Jesus burst out laughing. I couldn't help but join in.

Our laughter dissolved my fragmented mind.

2B
tuning forks

So it is that existence and nonexistence

each gives birth to the idea of the other;

difficulty and ease produce the idea of each other;

length and shortness each fashion the concept of the other;

height and lowness arise from the contrast of the one with the other;

musical notes become harmonious

through the relation of one with another;

and before and behind shape the meaning

of something following another.

"Before you are on the Path," said Lao Tzu, "you are in an either-or position. But once you are on the Path, you are both-and."

We had just come from a good meal, and now we were wandering Flagstaff's maze of alleys. Lao Tzu paused to pick his teeth while leaning against the alley's brick wall.

"These are two different worlds. As a human, you are two halves looking to operate as a whole. You look to 'put your best foot forward.' You have 'on the one hand and on the other hand.' You live in the either-or world." He gave a satisfied belch and scratched his belly. "But you are also a sphere of boundless energy with its center at your core. Your core is a dynamic pulsing, a condensing and expanding of energetic life. This is the both-and world."

Jesus nodded. "This is what I mean by 'I am in the Father and the Father is in me.' When a person knows this, she's in the both-and world. This is the second birth."

An idea struck me. "Oh, I get it! It's like being a tuning fork." I held up my arms over my head. "The fork has two branches—either-or. But when they're struck and set to vibrating, the fork is both-and."

Lao Tzu and Jesus chuckled, and we resumed our evening walk.

2c
nothing doing

Therefore the wise person
manages her affairs without doing anything,
and conveys her instructions without saying anything.
All things spring up, and not one refuses to show itself;
they grow and make no claim for their ownership;
they go through their processes,
and there is no expectation of reward.
The work is accomplished,
without any sense of achievement.

We walked from downtown to a little pond, where the three of us sat on a bench. Wedged comfortably between Jesus and Lao Tzu, I watched an osprey circling over our heads.

Jesus said, "Imagine a light above the crown of your head coming down through the midsection of your body and extending out your sacrum and your tailbone."

As he said the words, I could see and feel this line of light moving through me.

He continued, "This is the middle place. It is neither right nor left and yet is both right and left. All opposites are transcended here while at the same time being fully realized."

"Yes!" Lao Tzu gave his head an emphatic nod. "This is the place of your Real Eye Zing!"

Jesus laughed and groaned at the same time.

"I get it," I said. "When I operate from here," I gestured toward the invisible line of light that went through me, "when I am this, I cling to nothing while I'm fully immersed in everything. I am fully engaged while not attached."

Lao Tzu leaned across me and said to Jesus. "I think we may have to give him a Tao name."

"Hmm. What might that be?" asked Jesus.

"Nothing Doing," said Lao Tzu.

The osprey splashed into the water and came up with a fish.

3A

no muck, no rose

Rivalry is avoided

when those with superior ability are not admired;

thieves have no motivation

when one thing is not valued more than another;

people's minds will be at peace

if they are not excited by desire.

"The legs are not in competition with each other," mused Lao Tzu as we sat in the stands above the track, watching Flagstaff runners in their evening practice. "If we honored only one leg," he continued, "the other leg would succumb to leg envy. Running, even walking, would become impossible. Instead, the legs realize they are joined with a larger body. They run as one."

The three of us sat in silence for a moment as we considered Lao Tzu's imagery.

"One of my favorite Zen sayings," I said, "is that the Buddha is a shit stick."

Lao Tzu laughed. "Yes. It's all an interflow. Setting something up is a setup. Roses grow out of muck. No muck, no rose."

"Don't just love a piece of it. Love it all," said Jesus. "And what is doing the loving is what is being loved."

The setting sun threw light on the clouds, and they conjoined in dancing color.

We loved it.

3B

a star shot through the heavens

Therefore, when the wise person leads,

he empties the minds of his followers,

fills their bellies, weakens their wills,

and strengthens their bones.

He keeps everyone in no-knowledge and no-desire,

so that no one he knows dares not act.

Act by no-action.

Then, everything is in order.

We were lying on our backs in a grassy alpine meadow gazing at the planets and the stars. I found myself gratefully aware that I was embraced by the earth and not allowed to go flying into space.

"Surrender," said Jesus thoughtfully. "That's both what I had to do and what I chose to do."

"You followed the will of your Father," said Lao Tzu.

"Yes," said Jesus. "What you call moving with the Tao."

They know each other's language quite well, I thought to myself. They are of the same spirit, the same life force. They just express themselves in different terminology.

"I admire you deeply," said Lao Tzu. "Surrender is not an easy thing to do."

Jesus chuckled. "Well, I sweat blood over it. Part of me didn't want to surrender. I asked, if possible, that I not have to take the route of the Father's will, the way the Tao was unfolding."

They were silent for a while.

Finally, I said, "We're glad you did, Jesus. You followed through. All the way. You showed us the way to go."

"The word for non-action is 'wu-wei,'" said Lao Tzu. "The wu way. The way of being nothing in yourself so that the Source may come sourcing."

"Not my will but thine be done," said Jesus. I sensed he was speaking from his heart.

As we looked up into the night sky, a shooting star flashed across the darkness.

4

my cup runs over

The Tao is like the emptiness of a vessel;

and as we use it, we must be on our guard against all fullness.

How deep and unfathomable it is,

as if it were the honored ancestor of all things!

We should blunt our sharp points,

and unravel all the complications;

we should soften the glare of our brightness,

and bring ourselves into agreement with the obscurity of others.

How pure and still the Tao is,

as if nothing could ever change it!

I do not know whose child it is.

It seems possible it was here before Creation.

We were in my kitchen, where I had just made a fresh pot of coffee.

"May I pour you some?" asked Lao Tzu.

I held out my cup. "Sure."

He filled my cup . . . and kept pouring. The coffee spilled out onto the table.

"Stop!" I jumped up and grabbed a cloth to mop up the mess.

"The value of a cup is its emptiness," he said. "When it is full, it is worthless."

"No! No!" I was only half listening as I cleaned up his mess. "Its fullness is its value."

Lao Tzu laughed. "You prove my point. You are so full of yourself you cannot hear what I am saying. You are edgy and irritable. Your mind is tangled, yet you think of yourself as bright."

He was right, though I hated to admit it. I was upset with his overpouring. But his antics pointed to something deeper.

Meanwhile, Jesus had been leaning against my kitchen counter, watching us with a grin on his face. Now he said, "We must be empty in order to be filled. The emptying and filling are continuous. We are a running stream, a continuous flow of spirit. The life force."

Lao Tzu nodded. "Unlike the cup, you are a conduit. When you open to the Tao flow, your cup has no bottom."

"And no sides as well," said Jesus. "Vast openness extends in all directions."

As he spoke these words, my kitchen faded away. All walls fell. We sat open to the vastness of the One existing before all creation.

5A
the piñata of life

Heaven and earth are not motivated by kindness;

they deal with all things the way grass dogs are treated.

Wise men don't worry about benevolence;

they deal with people the same way they deal with grass dogs.

"I once caught a vision of God as blood-fanged with smiling eyes," I said one day as the three of us stood watching children at a birthday party. "He said he loves us so much he could eat us up." I shook my head. "And he does."

Lao Tzu shrugged. "Everything comes and goes. It serves whatever purpose it might have and moves on. Humans included."

"Yes," agreed Jesus. "I myself came to cast fire on the world. It was getting stagnated, more smoke than fire. We needed more fire, the fire of the everlasting flow of spirit."

"No destruction, no construction," said Lao Tzu.

For a moment, we silently watched the birthday party. A blindfolded child was taking swings with a stick at a piñata. The piñata was beautiful.

The child did not care.

Wham! The piñata split open, broken.

Treasure went everywhere.

5B
talk

Can't we compare the space between sky and earth to a bellows?

It's emptied, and yet it doesn't lose its power.

The more it moves, the more air it makes.

Talking too much, however, leads to a quick exhaustion.

Instead, guard your inner being and keep it free.

"As soon as you talk," said Lao Tzu, "you are dead!"

"You are dead!" I exclaimed.

Jesus said, ". . ."

The three of us sat on the mountain's saddle, gazing across a vast landscape spread out before us. We moved out of time. Our souls became as one.

No word was spoken.

6
a hint of existence

The valley spirit dies not; it is always the same.

We call it the feminine mystery.

Her gate is called the root from which grew heaven and earth.

Long and unbroken its power remains.

Use it with the gentlest touch.

Jesus, Lao Tzu, and I ambled down the Flagstaff street in the companionable silence of good friends who don't need to talk to enjoy each other's company. We paused on the sidewalk to watch the completion of a new doughnut shop.

"Hmm," said Lao Tzu. "What makes a doughnut a doughnut?"

"Is this a trick question?" I asked.

Jesus gave a little smile. "What is the value of my tomb?"

Lao Tzu clapped his hands. "Correct!"

I was confused . . . and then my mind opened. "Emptiness!"

We looked at each other. We smiled.

And then we moved on.

7
detached

Heaven is enduring and Earth continues long.

The reason why? They do not live of—or for—themselves.

This is how they are able to continue and endure.

Therefore the wise person puts herself last,

and she is foremost.

She treats herself with detachment,

and yet she continues.

She has no personal and private goals,

and therefore all her goals are accomplished.

The three of us were sitting on a bench by the pond. I held in my hand a small rock I had picked up on our walk. The rock's shape pleased me as I turned it over between my fingers.

"Hold that rock against my shoulder," said Lao Tzu.

I saw a flash of amusement in Jesus' eyes as I pressed the rock to Lao Tzu's shoulder.

Meanwhile, Lao Tzu leaned across me and began a deep conversation with Jesus about the Unborn and how all arose from It. Jesus called it the Wellspring. Their words continued, and my arm began to tremble. The small rock in my hand had grown heavier than I had thought it could be.

Finally, I blurted, "Lao Tzu, this is exhausting."

Lao Tzu nodded. "Holding something against someone always is."

"Yes," Jesus agreed. "Holding yourself against the entire Universe is especially tiring."

I let it go.

8
be like water

The highest excellence is like water.

Waters benefits all things without striving to do anything.

It is equally content to flow into the low places

that people ignore or dislike.

Therefore, water is like the Tao.

A home is excellent when it suits its inhabitants;

A mind is excellent when it is empty and open.

Companions are excellent when they are actively good.

Governments are excellent when they achieve order.

Movement is excellent when it is needed.

And when the most important person

doesn't complain if he is overlooked,

no one finds fault with him.

Lao Tzu held a bowl of water. "Watch." He poured the water into a glass, and then he turned to me. "What did you see?"

"I saw you pouring water."

"And?"

I scratched my beard. "Well, the water changed shape."

"Excellent!" He gave me his wide smile. "Water takes the shape of its container."

I shifted from one foot to another, a little uneasy with the point he was making.

"Don't worry," said Jesus, reading my mind. "You won't be a hypocrite. Water is always itself. It just completely fills the situation it is in."

"Do you know that game of rock, paper, scissors?" asked Lao Tzu.

I nodded.

"Always choose water."

9

Velcro mind

If you fill a bucket to the brim,

it's bound to spill when you carry it.

If you keep filing a point that's already sharp,

the point is sure to break.

When treasures fill the building,

they can't be kept safe long.

When wealth and honor lead to arrogance, evil follows.

When the work is done,

and you're starting to feel proud,

step back into obscurity

if you want to find the way of Heaven.

One morning as I was writing down my last conversation with Jesus and Lao Tzu, they both burst into my room.

"Here he is," said Lao Tzu to Jesus. "Mister Velcro Mind."

"He is one lost sheep," said Jesus.

"Please," I said. "Be quiet a minute. I'm trying to get this done."

Lao Tzu grinned. "Now he's stuck in annoyance."

Jesus nodded. "He's feeling righteous."

I sighed and tried to finish the sentence I was writing.

"Oh-oh," said Lao Tzu. "He's coming unglued."

"Well, that's good," said Jesus.

I threw up my hands and laughed. "I give up. I can't write this."

"You're too attached," said Jesus.

"Full of it," said Lao Tzu.

"Let's go for a walk," said Jesus.

"Just a minute." I wrote our conversation, my fingers flying over the keyboard. Then I stepped back from the computer. "Well, at least it's done."

"Ready?" Lao Tzu asked.

I nodded and followed them out the door. "Where are we going?"

"Serenity," said Lao Tzu.

10

the supreme virtue

When your mind-soul and your animal-soul

embrace each other, they become unified.

When you give your mind's undivided attention to your body's breath,

your mind becomes completely pliant, like a newborn child's.

When you wash your imagination, you become flawless.

Can you love and lead others

while letting go of your own goals?

Can you open and shut your interior gates of heaven,

as gently as a female bird flies?

While your intelligence reaches in every direction,

can you appear to know nothing?

The Tao creates all things and nourishes them;

it gives birth to them and yet does not claim them as its own.

It does all, and it yet does not boast of its deeds.

It presides over all, and yet it controls nothing.

This is what is called "the mysterious quality."

The three of us lingered on the sidewalk, observing a construction site. Then Lao Tzu walked up to the chain link fence and shook it.

"Let me out! Let me out!" he yelled.

One of the construction workers shouted back at him, "You are out!"

"Let me in! Let me in!" yelled Lao Tzu in reply.

Jesus said, "When you make the inside as the outside and the outside as the inside, you are in the Kingdom."

The walls inside my mind collapsed.

"Free," said Lao Tzu.

"And expensive," said Jesus. "It costs you everything."

We walked on. Lao Tzu began singing "Don't Fence Me In."

I laughed. What am I going to do with these guys?

11

running on empty

> The thirty spokes unite in a single hub,
>
> but the wheel's usefulness relies on the empty space for the axle.
>
> Clay is fashioned into vessels,
>
> but their usefulness is the hollowness within them.
>
> The door and windows are cut from walls to form a place to live,
>
> but people live in the empty space within.
>
> Positive existence can be purposefully adapted,
>
> but actual usefulness relies on nonexistence.

We sat drinking coffee at a sidewalk table. "'Wu,'" said Lao Tzu, "is the Chinese word for emptiness." He slurped his coffee. "Out of emptiness all things arise."

Jesus set his mug down on the table. "Some of the angels call my Father the Grand Empt for that very reason."

"'Chi,'" continued Lao Tzu, "is the word for the life force that fills all things, all forms."

"Like the Holy Spirit," I said.

Jesus gave me a smile. "Good Christian boy."

I turned to Lao Tzu, hoping to earn a smile from him as well. "'Ku' is the Japanese word for emptiness."

"Empty, filled, empty, filled!" the Old Dude exclaimed. "Wu Chi, Ku Chi. Wu Chi, Ku Chi!" He jumped to his feet and began to dance. "Come on, guys! Dance the Wu Chi Ku!"

Jesus and I joined him, and the three of us danced down the sidewalk. Passersby burst out laughing.

12
cradle and all

Color's five hues blind the eyes.

Music's five notes deafen the ears.

The mouth's five flavors deaden the sense of taste.

The pace of life—the mad hunt—drives the mind insane.

Desire distorts action.

Therefore the wise person seeks

to satisfy the belly's physical emptiness,

rather than the eye's insatiable longing.

He chooses his body's actual needs over his imagination's.

I yawned. "It's been fun, guys, but I have to go to sleep."

Jesus sat down on the floor of my bedroom. "We'll tell you a bedtime story."

Lao Tzu settled himself cross-legged beside Jesus. "Once upon a time," he said, "there was a glass of water that thought it was the glass."

"Once upon a time," said Jesus, "there was a wound that thought it was its bandage."

"Once upon a time there was an open heart that knew no bounds," said Lao Tzu. "Look, I think he's starting to drift off."

"When the body drops," asked Jesus, "who are you?"

"Hey!" Lao Tzu shouted. "That's my line!"

"Now look what you've done," Jesus said. "You woke him back up."

"That's our job," said Lao Tzu.

Jesus laughed. Then they pulled the blankets off me and left me, wide awake and uncovered.

13
a piece of the action

Favor and disgrace are equally dangerous;

honor and calamity present the same challenges.

What do we mean when we talk about disgrace and favor?

Disgrace is the low position where we find ourselves

after we've enjoyed favor.

Being favored makes us worry about losing our new importance;

our reputation is more vulnerable than it was before.

This is what we mean when we say

favor and disgrace are equally dangerous.

And what do we mean when we say

honor and great calamity are similar?

The thing that makes me vulnerable to calamity

is my body (the thing I call "myself").

If I had no body, what calamity could come to me?

Therefore, within your sphere of power,

honor everything and everyone

the way you would your own body.

Administer all the things

with which you have been entrusted

with the same love you have for your own person.

Jesus handed me a miniature ladder. "Climb to the top."

I looked down at the toy I held between my two hands. "I am already there."

"So fall to the bottom," said Lao Tzu.

"The bottom is in the palm of my hand," I said.

"At the top of the ladder," Jesus said, "is all your hope."

"At the bottom," said Lao Tzu, "is total disaster."

I looked at the small space between my two hands, and I burst out laughing.

"Why are you laughing?" asked Lao Tzu. "Don't you want to be a success?"

Jesus held out his hand. "Give me the ladder."

I handed it to him, and he bent it into a circle, melding

its bottom and its top together. "There!" he said. "An eternal hamster wheel." He threw it into the air.

It disappeared.

"What's for lunch?" asked Lao Tzu.

14
the Taoist third degree

We look at it, and we do not see it.

We name it Sameness.

We listen to it, and we do not hear it,

so we name it the Inaudible.

We try to grasp it, and we can't get hold of it,

so we name it the Subtle.

With these three qualities, we cannot describe it,

and so we blend them together.

And we have the One.

Its upper part is not light,

and its lower part is not dark.

Its action is ceaseless, yet it cannot be named.

It returns and becomes nothing.

This is called the Form of the Formless,

and the Appearance of the Invisible.

This is called the Fleeting and the Endless.

We meet it but we do not see its front;

we follow it, but we do not see its back.

When we can grasp the Tao of old

to direct the things of the present day,

when we know it as it was of old in the beginning,

this is called unwinding Tao's clue.

I was sitting by myself, trying to find God, when Lao Tzu ambled into my room. He leaned his face close to mine. "Show me your reputation," he whispered.

"Don't mess with me right now," I said.

"You do have one, don't you?"

"I suppose."

He poked me in the ribs.

I sighed. "All right, yes! Yes, I do!"

"Where is it?"

"In the minds of others."

"Where are the minds of others?"

"All scattered, I guess."

He poked me again.

"I don't know!"

"Does your reputation exist?" he persisted.

"Yes."

"Can you see it?"

"No, but I see its effects."

"Can you hear it?"

"No, but I hear talk about it."

"Can you hold it in your hand?"

"Of course not!"

"But it exists?"

"Yes!"

Jesus joined us then. He glanced at my face. "What's the matter with him?"

"He's trying to find God."

"Oh my," said Jesus.

"And he can't refute his repute," added the Old Dude.

Jesus shook his head. "The kingdom of heaven is like leaven."

"There's the clue," said Lao Tzu. "Let's leave him to unwind it."

15
total abandon

In the old times, the skillful masters of the Tao,

with subtle and exquisite insight,

comprehended its mysteries,

so deeply that they eluded the knowledge of others.

Since they were beyond others' knowledge,

I will make an effort to describe them.

They were hesitant,

like those who wade through an icy stream in winter;

cautious, like those who are constantly on guard;

respectful, as though they were always guests;

and without permanent boundaries, like melting ice.

They were as genuine as uncut wood,

empty as a valley, and opaque like muddy water.

How does cloudy water become clear?

When it is absolutely still,

the cloudiness gradually settles.

Who can make it come to rest?

If you let movement simply flow forward,

the condition of rest will gradually arise.

They who follow this method of the Tao

are not full of themselves.

Since they are not full of themselves,

they can afford to seem worn.

They have no need to appear new and complete.

"Come with me," said Jesus.

We climbed up to a meadow overlooking the town and sat on the ground. After a few minutes of silence, I asked, "How did you do it, Jesus?"

"Breath by breath," he said. "When I breathed in, I breathed in God's love. When I breathed out, I breathed out loving-kindness to the Earth and all who are on Earth."

"No matter the situation?" I asked.

Before Jesus could answer, Lao Tzu walked across the meadow and sat beside me.

"What about when you couldn't feel God's love?" I asked Jesus.

"You mean when I was on the cross?"

I nodded.

"Then I breathed in all the poisons and evils on Earth and breathed out loving-kindness and healing."

Lao Tzu sucked in a deep breath. "Like this." He let out his breath.

We sat there together, breathing in love, breathing out love; breathing in the poisons from the town below, breathing out loving-kindness and healing.

All around us grew calm and still.

16

returning to my destiny

Seek utter emptiness.

Guard stillness with tireless vigor.

Everything becomes active,

and then returns to its original state of stillness.

After green plants display their luxuriant growth,

they return to their roots.

This is stillness.

It indicates that the plants

have fulfilled their destiny.

This fulfillment is the unchanging rule.

To know this unchanging rule is to be wise;

not knowing it leads to chaos and evil.

Knowing this rule produces great capacity and patience.

Capacity and patience in turn create

a sense of connection with all reality.

From this sense of connection grows a royal character,

and the person whose character is royal

goes on to become Heaven-like.

When she is like Heaven, she possesses the Tao,

and now she can endure until her death,

with no fear of decay.

I sat alone, Jesus and Lao Tzu nowhere in sight. No bounds. No limits. Vast openness.

I heard their voices before I saw them, and then there they were, standing in front of me.

"Time to make yourself up," said Lao Tzu.

"Got to get an agenda," said Jesus.

"Shape up or ship out," said Lao Tzu.

"Get up on the cross of existence," said Jesus.

"Rise and shine," said Lao Tzu.

"It's your turn up to bat," said Jesus.

I sighed and stood up. "What's the matter?"

"You are!" They said the words in unison, and then both of them burst into laughter.

"We don't matter anymore," Lao Tzu said. "It's your turn."

I must have looked worried, because Jesus put his hand on my shoulder. "Don't worry. We are with you in spirit."

"You've got real potential, boy," said Lao Tzu. "And potential creates patience, patience creates connection, connection creates endurance, and endurance gets you to your destiny."

"'Testing achieves patience' is how one of my followers put it," said Jesus. "'Patience yields endurance, and endurance brings you to completion.'"

Lao Tzu pointed a finger at me. "Just remember one thing."

"What's that?"

"Stand up straight! Don't slump!"

17

moving with what is

In the old days, people weren't aware they had rulers.

Later, people loved their rulers and praised them.

Later yet, they feared them, and then they despised them.

When the rulers lost faith in the Tao,

people lost faith in their rulers.

Those earliest rulers were willing to be in the background.

Their willingness to be invisible,

showed they put more importance on their rule than on themselves!

Their work was done and their undertakings were successful,

while the people thought to themselves,

"We are as we are, naturally, all by ourselves!"

One clear, cool evening, the three us watched while people danced to a lively band in the open square downtown.

"The best dancing partner," mused Jesus, "is the one whom you hardly know is there."

I nodded. "And yet is responsive to your every move."

"Like the Tao. Or," Lao Tzu tipped his head toward Jesus, "like God the Father, in your language."

"When people are in that state," Jesus said, "when they are dancing with the Tao, that is the ultimate spiritual condition."

"Beyond that, it's all downhill," said Lao Tzu. "They start loving God, separating God out from everything else. Then they move to fearing God. They end up full of nothing but scorn."

"No more dancing with the Tao," said Jesus.

We stood silently for a while. A question occurred to me, and I turned to Jesus. "What church do you belong to?"

He smiled. "The church of Is."

Without another word, as though it were the most natural thing in the world, the three of us stepped onto the dance floor.

18
drooling on the pillow

When the Great Way ceased to be observed,

benevolence and righteousness came into vogue.

Next came knowledge and shrewdness,

followed by great hypocrisy.

When harmony no longer prevailed in the family,

loyal sons and daughters stepped up to claim their importance.

When the country fell into disorder,

patriotism appeared on the scene.

"It's kind of like reverse evolution," said Jesus.

Lao Tzu nodded. "Devolution."

"Devil-ution," said Jesus.

Lao Tzu waved a hand. "Whatever."

But Jesus was on a roll, and he clearly had more to say. "First you are in love. You have that glow, that oceanic feeling. The entire Cosmos is singing with joy, and your love knows no bounds."

"Ah," said Lao Tzu, nodding. "And then you live together."

"You notice she drools on the pillow," said Jesus.

"She notices you leave the seat up."

"The Great Tao of oceanic love is forgotten."

"And now," said Lao Tzu, "knowledge and shrewdness show up."

"You become very patriotic about it all. Or matriotic."

"Whatever," said Lao Tzu. "The Great Fish is now in a little pond."

"What's the answer?" I asked. "What's the way out?"

Jesus and Lao Tzu looked at each other and grinned. "Tango!" Together, they spiraled into the heavens.

19
chain of fools

If we could let go of our wisdom,

things would go much better.

If we could renounce our kindness

and discard our righteousness,

we could get back to being respectful and loving.

If we could stop scheming and worrying about the profit margin,

theft would disappear.

These methods of living lack worth.

Instead, return to integrity and authenticity.

Give up selfishness.

Renounce desire.

"Stand right there," said Jesus to me. "Without you there would be no performance. You're the audience."

"Why do I have to be the bad guy?" asked Lao Tzu.

"Out of character for me," said Jesus. "You'll be more believable."

"Fine." Lao Tzu rolled his eyes. "Go ahead then. Say your lines."

"They are not mere lines," Jesus said. "They are the truth."

"So is that your first line?"

"See." Jesus pointed his finger at Lao Tzu. "I told you. You make a great bad guy."

"Fine," Lao Tzu said again. "Let's get started."

Jesus turned to me, "You are a prayer calling out."

Lao Tzu held out his hand to me. "Here's some money. Hope that helps."

"You are a soul thirsty for living water," said Jesus.

"Here is the chatter of your mind," Lao Tzu said. "Drink some of that."

"You are a heart yearning for home," said Jesus.

"Distract yourself," said Lao Tzu. "Drive around. Shop. Eat."

"Live from the core of your being."

"Wear the social armor you have forged for yourself."

"Be attached to nothing," said Jesus. "If they ask for your coat, give them your shirt too."

"Take the bastards to court."

"Wow!" I said. "What's the name of this play?"

"The Chain of Fools," said Lao Tzu.

20
saints and rockets

Give up learning, and you'll have no more worries.

When it comes to being compliant and being ingratiating,

there's not much difference between the two.

Pay attention to what their consequences are.

How much distance between them is there really after all?

What everyone fears is fearful;

but how wide and without end

is the range of questions asking to be discussed!

Everyone around me looks satisfied and pleased;

as if they were enjoying a full banquet,

as if they were standing on top a tower in spring.

I alone seem listless and still,

like a baby who hasn't yet learned to smile.

My desires haven't yet made me aware of their presence.

I look dejected and forlorn, as if I had no home to go to.

Everyone else seems to have enough and to spare.

I alone seem to have lost everything.

My mind is stupid; I am in a state of chaos.

Ordinary people look bright and intelligent,

while I alone seem to be cloudy and dim.

They seem to be full of discrimination,

while I alone am dull and confused.

I seem to be carried about as on the sea,

drifting as if I had nowhere to rest.

Everyone else has a sphere of action,

while I alone seem dull and incapable, aimless.

I am different from everyone else,

but I value the nourishment of the Tao's mother-milk.

"What is a saint?" I asked Jesus.

He looked up at the sky. "A rocket is essentially propulsion and expansion. As a rocket, so a saint."

I scratched my beard and waited, hoping for more.

Lao Tzu took pity on me. "Your expansion depends on your fuel that propels you." He gave me one of his knowing sideways glances. "A moment ago, you were fueled by a desire for a piece of cherry pie. That desire produced a certain expansion of awareness."

"Well," Jesus said, "a limited expansion. What you might call a small cherry-pie aura."

I looked back and forth between them. "What are you fueled by?"

"Our Source, our Origin, our Father," said Jesus promptly.

"The Tao," Lao Tzu said, "the Path, the Way, our Mother."

I thought about that for a moment. "I call it the Wellspring," I said.

"That's okay," said Lao Tzu. "The name is not It."

"When propelled by the Infinite," Jesus said, his gaze following a cloud that was drifting across the blue sky, "our expansion is Infinite."

I watched the cloud with him for a moment. "That's what you mean by 'I and my Father are one,'" I said finally.

"You got it!"

"All right all ready!" Lao Tzu whirled in a circle, then did a cartwheel. Cavorting like a child released from school, he sang, "Dancing with the Tao."

After a moment, Jesus and I joined in.

21

this

The Tao is the source of all activity.

But who can explain it?

It can neither be touched or seen,

and yet it contains the shapes of everything,

the essence of all.

It is deep, dark, and obscure;

the truth of all reality is contained within it.

As it was, it is still.

Its name endures.

And within it no beginning is lost.

How do I know that this is so?

By this.

I was sleeping soundly when Lao Tzu yanked the covers off me. "Rise and shine!"

I groaned, rolled over, and opened one eye. The clock said 2:27 a.m. "All right," I sighed and stumbled to my feet. "Where's Jesus?"

"Outside." He opened the door. "Let's go."

We found Jesus looking up at the stars and moon.

"Point at the moon," Lao Tzu commanded me.

I pointed.

"Now," he said, "let the back wall of your mind fall away."

I let it.

"Who is doing the pointing?" he asked.

I laughed. "There is no point. There is only this."

We stood silently, within the Cosmos, as the Cosmos. No boundaries. No bounds.

22

let it go

The partial becomes complete;

the crooked, straight; the empty, full;

the worn out, new.

The person with few desires gets what she wants;

The person who wants everything goes off course.

Therefore the wise person holds in his embrace one thing,

and manifests it to all the world.

He is free from self-display, and therefore he shines;

from self-assertion, and therefore he is distinguished;

from self-boasting,

and therefore his merit is acknowledged;

from self-complacency,

and therefore he acquires superiority.

It is because he is free from striving

that no one can strive against him.

The old saying that "the partial becomes complete"

is not an empty phrase.

All real completion comes from letting go.

The next day we were sitting in the grass in the park watching some folk doing Tai Chi.

Lao Tzu scrambled to his feet. "Here is how you move with chi." He took a step. "For the left foot to go forward, the right foot must push backward. To go forward, you have to go backward." He took a step back. His left foot pushed forward and his right foot moved back. "To go backward, you must direct your energy forward."

Jesus watched him thoughtfully. "If you wish to be reborn into the next step, you must let yourself die to your old stance."

"Exactly." Lao Tzu dropped back onto the grass beside me. "It is called emptying and filling."

"I see." I got to my feet and tried it for myself. "If I want to open to everything, I have to give everything up. I have to let it all go."

Lao Tzu looked at Jesus. "The boy might amount to something yet."

Jesus nodded. "As long as he keeps being good for nothing."

The three of us burst into laughter.

23

surrender

The person who speaks little stays true to herself.

Strong winds don't last all morning,

and a cloudburst doesn't last all day.

What makes this so? Sky and earth.

If sky and earth cannot make weather last more than a day,

why should a person expect her emotions to endure much longer?

Follow the Tao, and you will be with the Tao.

Follow virtue, and you will be with virtue.

Let things go, and you will be with surrender.

The Tao welcomes all those who follow it.

Virtue welcomes all those who follow it.

Surrender welcomes all those who are willing to let go.

But those who do not trust the Way,

will not earn others' trust.

Later that day, we were sitting at the back table of a local diner. Lao Tzu was having tea, I had a cup of hot black coffee in front of me, and Jesus was sipping a glass of water.

Jesus set his glass down on the table. "You have a right and a left, a front and a back. What is in the middle?"

"Room." Lao Tzu crooked his little finger as he lifted his cup to his lips. "Capaciousness," he added after he had taken a swallow. "Like your glass of water has room for the water."

I looked down into my coffee cup. "The space inside me condenses and expands. Sometimes I am full of me and there is no room at all."

"No room, no Tao flow," said Lao Tzu.

"No room, no Spirit flow," said Jesus. "See that person?" He nodded his head toward a woman who had just entered the diner. "She is going through great loss. She is suffering."

I turned and looked. "She doesn't look it."

Lao Tzu nodded. "That is because she is not bitter or angry, not depressed and defeated."

"The suffering of her loss is making room," explained Jesus. "She is surrendering and opening."

"She will be fine." Lao Tzu met Jesus' eyes and nodded. "The Christ Child will be born within her because she has room in the In."

Jesus laughed. "And quoting some Old Guy, 'The Tao welcomes all those who follow it.'"

24
only be

He who stands on his tiptoes does not stand firm;

she who tries to stretch her stride does not walk easily.

he who tries to get others to notice him does not shine;

she who asserts her own views is not distinguished;

he who boasts does not find his merit acknowledged;

she who is conceited has no authority.

Viewed from the standpoint of the Tao,

these attitudes are like food-stained clothing,

or a tumor on the body—

something unnecessary and unappealing.

That's why the person who follows the Tao

is simply himself, without pretense.

That night, just as I climbed into bed, Jesus and Lao Tzu came to tuck me in.

I looked back and forth between them. "Tell me a bedtime story."

"Well." Jesus looked at Lao Tzu.

"Once upon a time."

"There was a musical note," said Jesus.

"It was B," said Lao Tzu.

"Sometimes B tried to B sharp."

"In trying to B sharp, it B came flat."

They fell silent and just stood there, looking at me.

"I guess I should just B," I said.

Lao Tzu slugged me with a pillow. "Wise guy!"

"Come on," Jesus said to him, and they left the room.

"Hey! Hey!" I shouted after them. "Turn out the light!"

25
the word

There was something undefined and complete,

coming into existence before Heaven and Earth.

How still it was and formless,

standing alone, and undergoing no change,

reaching everywhere and in no danger of ever being exhausted!

Think of it as the Mother of all things.

I do not know its name, so I call it the Tao, the Way.

If I try even harder to use words to describe it,

I call it only the Wonderful.

Wonderful, it passes on in constant flow.

Passing on, it becomes distant.

Having become distant, it returns.

Therefore the Tao is wonderful;

Heaven is wonderful; Earth is wonderful;

and the wise person is also wonderful.

In the universe there are four things that are wonderful,

and the wise person is one of them.

People take their law from the Earth;

the Earth takes its law from Heaven;

Heaven takes its law from the Tao.

The law of the Tao is simply what it is.

The three of us walked to the old church, the one with the gargoyles and the angels. We went in and sat down in a pew. The light shone through the colored windows, and we watched it silently.

Finally, I turned to Jesus who was sitting beside me "What is religion?"

"Story," he said. "In the beginning was the word."

Lao Tzu raised his bushy eyebrows. "And before the beginning?"

They looked across me and smiled at each other.

"But which story do I believe?" I asked.

"The story that is large enough to contain you without your being contained," said Jesus.

I sighed. "You guys always speak in paradoxes and parables."

"Definitely," said Lao Tzu.

"Infinitely," said Jesus.

For some reason, they thought that extremely funny. Their laughter was contagious. By the time we left the church, we were all chuckling.

"Excellent service," said Jesus.

26
going for a ride

Lightness can't exist without gravity.

Quietness is the master of restlessness

Therefore the wise person travels an entire day

without leaving beyond her supplies.

Even though she looks at luxurious sights.

she remains composed, indifferent.

How can someone who has many vehicles

take the world lightly?

Don't lose your grounding.

If you are restless, you lose your authority.

I was giving Jesus and Lao Tzu a ride in my older model Funk. Jesus was riding shotgun, while Lao Tzu was in the back seat.

"The best leader always follows behind," he'd murmured as he climbed in. Now, my Funk was plunging us down the mountain road at ever increasing speed.

Jesus watched the trees fly past. "What is at the core of you?"

I sighed. "A very heavy heart."

Lao Tzu leaned forward and stuck his head between Jesus and me. "That's why we are in this Funk." He put a hand on my shoulder. "Take some breaths and just be."

I began to move out of my head and into my breath.

The Funk slowed down.

Jesus told me a Jesus joke.

I groaned but I couldn't help but laugh. "Jesus, that's awful!"

The Funk became transparent, then disappeared. The three of sat on the road and looked at each other.

"Next time, maybe you'll give us a spin in your Tizzy," said Lao Tzu.

Jesus and I looked at each other. This time we both groaned.

Lao Tzu got to his feet and then held out a hand to each of us. He pulled us to our feet, and we walked together, side by side, back up the mountain.

27
heliotrope

The skillful traveler leaves behind no tracks;

the skillful speaker says nothing that gives offense;

the skillful reckoner doesn't keep a running tally;

the skillful closer needs no bolts or bars,

and yet to open what he has shut is impossible;

the skillful binder uses no strings or knots,

but to loosen what she has bound is impossible.

In the same way, the wise person is always skillful at saving others,

and so he never rejects anyone.

He can save all things,

and so he doesn't waste anything.

This is called using the light so you can accomplish all things.

Therefore, the skillful person teaches the unskilled

but those who are less skilled help her.

The one honors the other,

and the other is glad for her helper.

An intelligent observer might mistake their relationship.

It is a secret!

One afternoon, I went looking for Jesus and Lao Tzu. I found them in a meadow, looking at flowers. Lao Tzu was lying on his belly, chin in hands, and Jesus sat beside him.

Lao Tzu looked up at me. "These flowers move with the sun."

Jesus touched a red blossom. "They keep their faces turned toward the light."

"They are flow-ers," said Lao Tzu.

"What is the flower of your heart?" asked Jesus.

I thought a moment. "A petunia."

"Like a satellite dish!" said Lao Tzu.

"My heart flower is a rose," said Jesus.

Lao Tzu gave me a grin. "Mine's a snapdragon!" He leapt up and wrestled me to the ground.

Jesus leaned back on his elbows and watched us. "I swear. Sometimes I think you are both fourteen."

"Just drunk on the light," said Lao Tzu.

We got up and headed back to town.

28
last turtle standing

Know the strength of your masculinity,

while understanding the gentleness of your femininity;

Just as many streams flow into a single channel,

everything will come to you.

You will hold on to constant excellence,

as genuine as a child.

Be white,

yet allow yourself to be black.

This is humility the world will see,

a pattern for authenticity.

Know the shine of glory,

yet be happy to be disgraced.

You will walk in a wide valley,

and everyone will see your true being.

Unworked clay is willing

to be divided, distributed, and formed into vessels.

The wise person leads others,

and avoids violence in all she accomplishes.

One afternoon, we wandered into an empty classroom in the high school. I took a seat in one of the students' desks, and Jesus and Lao Tzu sat side by side behind the teacher's desk. Jesus wore a black mortarboard, tassel to the right; Lao Tzu wore a white mortarboard, tassel to the left.

Lao Tzu turned to Jesus. "You are wearing my hat."

"Oh!" Jesus took off his hat and handed it to Lao Tzu. Lao Tzu did the same. When both had settled their hats on their heads, they turned back to me.

"Now for your first and last question," said Lao Tzu. "They say it's turtles all the way down. If that is true, on what does the last turtle stand?"

I thought for a moment, but before I could come up with an answer, the bell rang for the end of the school day. Jesus and Lao Tzu jumped to their feet.

"Don't forget to do your homework!" said Jesus over his shoulder as he left the classroom.

"Where is home?" I called after them.

Lao Tzu paused in the doorway. "Congratulations!" he said. "You answered the question."

29
forcing my hand

If you want to control the world,

you'll never succeed.

The world is like the wind,

and you can never actively grasp it.

If you think you have hold of it,

actually, you've destroyed it.

When you think you have it in your hand,

really you've lost it.

Things that were once at the front

are now behind.

What was warm becomes cool.

Strength arises out of weakness,

and everything you've worked so hard

to achieve falls into ruin.

If you're wise, you'll avoid extremes.

You'll stay away from

both extravagance and over indulgence.

Early one morning, we were walking by the lake.

"Be in the world but not of the world," said Jesus.

I looked around me. "What is the world?"

"All that is under the sky," said Lao Tzu.

I let that sink in. After a moment, I said, "I don't like the world. I want to change it."

Jesus squatted by the lake and put his hand into the water. "Look." He cupped his fingers. "Is my hand in the water or the water in my hand?"

"Both," I said.

"Can my hand change the water?"

I saw his point, but I scrambled to find a logical argument.

Lao Tzu tossed a pebble at me.

"Ow!"

"Wake up!" he said. "Change the water in your own cup!"

"How do I do that?" I asked.

"Like this." Jesus uncupped his fingers, and the water flowed around his hand.

30
rebound

The one who follows the Tao doesn't use force to control others.

Using forces always backfires.

Armies aren't good for the land.

Famine follows warfare.

A wise person knows when to stop.

She doesn't keep pushing once she's proved her point.

She does what she has to do,

but she's careful not to be arrogant.

She takes necessary action

without clinging to her own power.

Anything that grasps its own strength and power too tightly,

inevitably wears out.

This is not the way of the Tao,

and what doesn't follow the Tao soon runs into trouble.

Later that afternoon, we walked along the banks of a river. I noticed a hefty stick on the ground, and I bent to pick it up. It was the size and arced shape of a samurai sword, so I gave it a little swing.

Jesus looked at me with compassion, but I noticed Lao Tzu had a glint in his eye.

Looking to test the stick's strength, I swung it with all my might at a tree limb in front of me. It rebounded with equal force and struck me in the forehead.

I staggered and saw stars.

Lao Tzu let out of a whoop of laughter. "All chi—" He was laughing so hard he couldn't get out the word. "All chi—" He tried again. "All chi—"

Jesus finished the phrase for him. "All chickens come home to roost!"

I put the stick back where I found it. I couldn't help but join their laughter.

31

rung three

Weapons, however beautifully crafted,

are instruments of evil.

All creatures hate them.

Therefore, those who follow the Tao do not use weapons.

Ordinarily, the wise person considers

the left hand—the feminine quality—the most honorable place,

but in time of war, people value more the right hand—the masculine quality.

Sharp weapons are instruments of evil, however,

and a wise person turns to them

only when they are absolutely necessary.

Instead, the wise person values calm and peace.

Victory through force is meaningless.

To think otherwise would mean

to delight in human slaughter.

The person who delights in slaughter

brings discord to the world.

In times of celebration, the masculine quality is prized.

During times of mourning, the feminine quality is valued.

The second-in-command of the army

has his place on the left,

while the general has his on the right,

a place of mourning.

The person who has killed in battle should weep

with bitterest grief for those who have lost their lives.

A victory in battle is like a funeral.

In my dream, Lao Tzu walked up to me with a pistol in his hand. "I have come to kill you," he said.

"What?" I exclaimed.

He sighed. "I will not rejoice in shooting you."

"A lot of good that does me," I said.

He nodded. "But I will be as sad as if I were at a funeral."

"Thanks a lot," I answered. "I'm so happy you have taken a step up on the evolutionary ladder."

"You." Jesus pointed to Lao Tzu. "Go to rung three."

"What's rung three?" I asked.

"If rung one is killing and rejoicing in the killing," Jesus answered, "then rung two is killing and being sad about it."

"And rung three?"

"Rung three is not killing."

Lao Tzu put the pistol in his pocket and said sadly, "So many humans never reach rung three."

"They are drunk," said Jesus. "One day they will sober up."

I woke up to find Jesus and Lao Tzu sitting on the foot of my bed. They were smiling at me.

32

wings

The unchanging Tao has no name.

Though in its primordial simplicity it may be small,

the whole world cannot command those who follow it.

The world spontaneously yields to any leader

who guards and holds it.

When Tao is followed,

Heaven and Earth unite

and sweet dew falls on the Earth,

a dew that reaches everyone, everywhere,

without any human help.

As soon as the Tao becomes active, it has a name.

When it once has that name,

human beings can know to rest in it.

When they know to rest in it,

they can be free from all risk of failure and error.

The relation of the Tao to all the world

is like that of the great rivers and seas

that fill the smaller streams.

The three of us were sitting on a bench at the pond, watching the birds: raven, osprey, heron, red-winged blackbird, swallow, duck.

After a while, Lao Tzu mused out loud: "What would a one-winged bird do?"

"Flutter helplessly on the ground," I said.

He nodded. "And if a two-winged bird chooses one wing over another?"

I tried to picture it. "It would fly round and round in circles."

"Someone gave me this the other day," Jesus said and pulled out of his pocket a small silver crucifix. "What if both wings were nailed here?"

"Immobilized suffering," said Lao Tzu.

"I much prefer the empty tomb," said Jesus. "Then your wings are in perfect flying order."

At that, I found myself ascending with them into the heavens like vapor. Then we condensed, dropped down as rain, became a river, flowed into the ocean, evaporated into the sky . . . and dropped down again. This time, we were in the form of three men sitting on a bench.

"You guys are so much fun," I said.

33

staying power

He who knows others is discerning,

but she who knows herself has true wisdom.

She who overcomes others is strong,

but he who overcomes himself is mighty.

He who is satisfied with his lot is rich,

and she who never gives up has power.

She who carries out her responsibilities to others

will endure long.

And he who is willing to die to this world

will live forever.

We were sitting on our favorite bench downtown, me in the middle. I could feel their shoulders against mine, solid and warm, which made me think.

"How come you guys are still alive," I asked. "Aren't you supposed to be dead?"

Jesus leaned across me to exchange a look with Lao Tzu. "Define dead," he said.

"No longer having a body," I answered.

"He is saying that only a body matters," said Lao Tzu to Jesus.

Jesus nodded. "He is saying that the physical body is all that is mattering."

"Hey!" I said. "I'm right here. Stop talking about me as though I weren't here!"

They looked at me.

"Which is more alive?" Jesus asked. "You or your clothes?"

"Me," I said.

"Well, why aren't you naked?" said Jesus.

My mind stopped.

"There," said Lao Tzu.

"Here," said Jesus.

34

one sun, three moons

All-pervading is the Great Tao!

It is found on the left hand and on the right.

All things depend on it for their being,

which it gives to them.

All things are obedient to it,

but it makes no claim on the work it accomplishes.

It clothes all things, but it possesses nothing.

It may be recognized in the smallest things.

All things return to their roots and disappear,

never knowing that the Tao presided over their entire lives.

It may be recognized in the greatest things.

Only through the Tao

does the wise person accomplish anything.

Only by being willing to be nothing,

do we achieve anything.

One morning I opened my eyes to find Jesus and Lao Tzu sitting cross-legged beside my bed. "You dreamed of two full moons in the sky," said Lao Tzu.

I rubbed my eyes. "Yes," I said. "I did."

"One is the Eastern way, the way of Tao," said Jesus.

"The other is the Western way, the way of Christianity," said Lao Tzu.

I yawned. "The two were in the sky," I said, "with a dove of peace etched in the clouds between them."

"The light of one reflects the other," said Jesus.

I sat up. "Some of your followers won't like that, Jesus. They want only one moon."

"In my father's house are many mansions," he said. "Besides, they should be looking at the Sun, not the moon."

I scratched my beard and thought about my dream. "There was a third full moon in the sky, forming an equal-sided triangle with the other two," I said. "What's that about?"

Jesus got to his feet. "We will talk about that when the time comes."

"Is it Islam?" I asked.

Lao Tzu burst out laughing, but Jesus just smiled. "Now you are really going to be in trouble."

35

a Tao sandwich

If you hold in your hands the Great Image

of the invisible Tao, the whole world is safe.

Others will follow you without coming to any harm.

In your presence, they'll find rest, peace, and a feeling of ease.

Music and good cooking will welcome guests into your presence.

If you try to talk about the Tao,

your words will seem insipid and flavorless.

You can't see it, can't hear it,

and yet you will never exhaust it.

Later that morning, I heard Lao Tzu in my kitchen singing, "Tao and Zen, there's a fool such as I."

I went to see what he was up to. "What are you doing?"

"I am making myself a Tao sandwich."

Jesus was leaning against the kitchen counter. "Are you making yourself into a sandwich?" he asked. "Or are you making a sandwich for yourself to eat?"

"Precisely," said Lao Tzu. He laid a slice of bread atop a slice of bread.

"Lao Tzu," I said, "there's nothing in the middle."

He nodded. "When there is nothing in the middle, there is room for everything."

"That is why I made myself of no reputation," said Jesus.

"If there was something in the middle," Lao Tzu added, "it would not be a Tao sandwich."

"What would it be?" I asked.

"A hero," said Lao Tzu.

"A sub-way," said Jesus.

"I have made myself both of those sandwiches." I eyed Lao Tzu's sandwich. "But I like the Tao sandwich better."

Lao Tzu shrugged. "I cannot make you one."

"You have to make yourself one," said Jesus.

"Or better still," said Lao Tzu, "make yourself nothing."

36

a drowning kitten

Before you can breathe in,

you must breathe out.

When you want to become weaker,

you must first allow yourself to become stronger.

If you want to conquer yourself,

first lift yourself up.

Before you can be humbled,

you must know your own worth.

This is called "hiding your light."

The soft overcomes the hard,

and the weak the strong.

Fish should be left to swim in deep water,

and people don't need to understand the means

to appreciate the results.

One afternoon, I sat at the computer, struggling to write my adventures with Jesus and Lao Tzu. Meanwhile, Lao Tzu and Jesus hovered behind me, reading over my shoulder, but I didn't know they were there.

"He is trying to write this without us," Jesus said softly.

"He is full of himself," whispered Lao Tzu.

"He is head strong and heart weak," said Jesus.

"His balloon will eventually burst."

"He is hard and fast on his way."

"Let's go even slower," suggested Lao Tzu. "Maybe he will eventually catch up."

"No chance," said Jesus. "He is in an entirely different dimension."

"Dementia," said Lao Tzu.

I sighed and pushed my chair back from the computer. "I give up."

"Finally," said Lao Tzu

"Welcome back," said Jesus.

I was surprised to see them standing there. "Where have you two been?"

They looked at each other. "We were trying to rescue a drowning kitten," said Lao Tzu.

"Is the kitten okay?" I asked.

Jesus grinned. "He is one strange cat."

"Well," I said, "I could have used your help. I was having a tough time writing."

I couldn't understand why they whooped with laughter.

37
nameless simplicity

> The Tao in its regular course
>
> does nothing for the sake of doing it,
>
> and so there is nothing it does not do.
>
> If the world's leaders could follow the Tao,
>
> all things would be transformed.
>
> If this transformation becomes something I desire,
>
> I will transform even the desire with a nameless simplicity.
>
> A simplicity without a name is free from all external aim.
>
> With no desire, it is at rest and still.
>
> Things will naturally take their proper course.

On a clear, cool day, the three of us had climbed Mount El-
den, and now we were sitting off the trail, each of us leaning
against a tree.

"So," asked Jesus, "are you ready for this?"

"I don't know," I answered.

"'Don't know' is always good," said Lao Tzu.

Jesus leaned over and put his hand on my shoulder. "I am closer to you than your very breath. I am inside you and you are inside me."

"The Tao of Tao," said Lao Tzu. "Interflow."

"Do you know how and what I am inside you?" Jesus asked me.

I shook my head.

"I am Imagination."

Lao Tzu nodded. "All is created through Imagination."

"Be still," said Jesus, "and know that you are Imagination."

"You are mage, you are magi," said Lao Tzu. "You are a mage-ician."

"The Christ Child you seek is born in Imagination," said Jesus. "He is Imagination."

"The Imagination does everything," said Lao Tzu. "And yet nothing is done."

"Imagination is the only Reality," said Jesus.

I scratched my beard. "Then who am I?"

"You are your imagination creating a side pocket in the ongoing flow of Imagination," said Jesus.

"Then you get all shook up," said Lao Tzu, "fearful and anxious, bold and demanding, seeking salvation."

"When you start naming yourself, you get in trouble," said Jesus.

"That's called black magic," said Lao Tzu. "It's loving the spin, loving the spin you are in. But we are looking for nameless simplicity."

"Let's start a new church," I said. "The Church of the Boundless Imagineers."

Lao Tzu groaned and exchanged looks with Jesus. "I knew he was trouble from the start."

We got up, stretched, and continued walking on the path of no path.

38
dejection and resurrection

People who follow the Tao keep quiet about it,

and therefore they possess the Tao fully.

People who have less awareness of the Tao,

try too hard to possess the Tao,

and therefore, they lose what little understanding they have.

Those who follow the Tao most closely do nothing

and have no need to do anything.

Those who are off-course from the Tao,

are always busy doing things,

as though that will get them back on track.

The kindest people naturally act in ways that are kind,

without any self-conscious striving to be kind.

Truly good people always seek to bring goodness to the world.

Those who sense what needs to be done,

roll up their sleeves and get busy.

They step up to the plate.

Even when the Tao was lost,

its way became clear.

When its way disappeared, kindness appeared.

When kindness was lost, righteousness appeared.

But when true righteousness was lost,

people started relying on morality.

Morality is faith's empty shell.

Chaos sets in when people rely on morality,

when they seek only the flower of the Tao,

rather than its essence.

Stick with what is solid.

Let go of what is flimsy.

Take the fruit rather than the flower.

Turn your back on the shell,

and choose the essence.

I sat dejected.

Lao Tzu folded his arms and watched me for a moment. Then he turned to Jesus. "He's down in the dumps."

"What's the matter?" Jesus asked me.

I sighed. "They say I am nothing but a pile of neurons yakking." I felt my shoulders slump a little lower. "And that there is no meaning, no God, no Tao, except what I invent."

"Who are 'they?'" Jesus asked. "If you go by 'their' definition, they're just another pile of neurons yakking!"

Lao Tzu poked me in the shoulder. "Why would you believe a pile of neurons yakking instead of us?"

I sat up straighter. I started to smile.

Jesus walked over to the window and looked out. "It's snowing," he said. "Let's go for a walk and listen to the snow fall."

As we went out the door, Lao Tzu asked me, "What is the sound of a snow flake falling?"

I didn't have an answer.

He gave me a smile. "Joy."

We walked through the silent snow.

All around us was the essence of beauty.

39

an advance

When things are in harmony with the Tao,

the sky is bright and pure,

and the earth is firm and solid.

Spirit is what it is meant to be.

Valleys' hollows are full of life,

and all creatures are healthy.

The world's leaders rely on the Tao as their model.

All these things come from the Tao's unity.

Without the Tao,

the sky becomes polluted,

the earth is unstable, and spirit fails.

Valleys are barren and dry,

creatures become extinct,

and governments fall.

Thus it is that dignity finds its deepest root in humility,

and what is lofty finds its stability

in the lowest depths from which it springs.

Wise leaders lay no claim on their family legacy,

and they make no self-righteous claim to goodness.

Their worth is built on their smallness

rather than their greatness.

They are willing to look like ordinary stones,

rather than fancy jade.

Late one night, I sat in my room mourning. I looked up when Jesus and Lao Tzu walked in. "Wake me when the world is over."

They exchanged a glance.

"He needs an advance," said Jesus.

I shook my head. "You mean a retreat."

"All retreat is an advance," said Lao Tzu.

Jesus held out his hand. "Come with us."

We walked out into the starry night.

I stood between them, staring up at the sky. "Why is there evil in the world?" I asked.

"Because there are humans in the world," Jesus answered.

"No humans, no evil," said Lao Tzu.

I sighed. "Why are we so stupid?"

Jesus shrugged. "Self-infatuation."

"The question is not 'Why?'" said Lao Tzu. "The question is 'How?'"

"How what?" I asked.

"How to be wise," he said.

"Regard the whole world as yourself," said Jesus.

"Condense it," Lao Tzu added, "put it in your pocket, and walk the Path."

"Move from your heart. Be willing to be small."

A shooting star blazed across the heavens.

40

knock, knock

The Tao returns as it goes forth.

Its strength is marked by weakness.

All that exists and is named

springs from the Tao.

Existence comes from that which is unnamed and nonexistent.

Lao Tzu called from outside my door, "Knock, knock!"

"The door is open," Jesus answered.

Lao Tzu stepped into the doorway. "The door is not-hinged."

Jesus nodded. "Yes, it is no-thing-ed."

"It is the gateless gate," said Lao Tzu.

"Nothing stands in your way," said Jesus.

Lao Tzu touched the doorway's empty space. "This is a serious obstacle."

I stood in my living room and watched my door opening and closing, yielding and returning.

Jesus turned to me. "You are the door."

"Become unhinged," said Lao Tzu.

"Become no-thing," said Jesus.

The door and the doorframe disappeared. All my mental framework fell away too. "Knock, knock." I rapped my knuckles on the air. Suddenly, the door was back again.

"Here we go again," said Lao Tzu.

"Your knocking creates the door," said Jesus.

"Who's there?" I asked.

"No one!" They laughed and spun me round and round until I didn't know whether I was coming or going.

"How do you step into a revolving door?" Lao Tzu called to Jesus as we whirled in circles.

"The same way you step out!"

41

spiritual power

When the wisest people hear about the Tao, they follow it.

People who have a little bit of wisdom try to stick to its path,

but they keep losing their way.

People who lack any wisdom,

when they hear about the Tao, burst out laughing.

If the Tao did not seem so amusing to those who lack wisdom,

it would not be the Tao.

That's why these sayings exist:

The path that leads toward the light is always dim.

We make progress by retreating.

The best way is always rough and long.

The way leads through empty valleys.

The way often seems to make no sense.

You travel best when you travel lightest.

You are most powerful

when you are gentle and humble.

The Tao never changes

and yet it always looks different.

The Tao is a square with no corners.

It is a great vessel that takes shape slowly.

It is loud but speaks not a word.

Its image is immense,

and yet it casts no shadow.

The Tao is hidden and has no name,

but it is the Tao that gives all things

what they need

and makes them complete.

"What do you think about weapons and the use of weapons?" I asked Jesus and Lao Tzu.

"I stick by what I wrote so long ago," said Lao Tzu. "Weapons are the tools of violence. All decent folk detest them."

Jesus nodded. "Physical power always fails. Spiritual power is the path to follow."

"The Marine Corps' manual agrees with you," I said.

"What does it say?" asked Lao Tzu.

"Unless you conquer the spirit of people, you have not won the war."

"You can never conquer the spirit of people," said Jesus.

"The Way and its power seems weak to the foolish," said Lao Tzu. "But it always wins. And why? Because it does not play the win-lose game."

I thought I understood what he meant, so I ventured to say, "Embodying the spirit of the Life Force means you have no death to die."

"When you have no death to die, you have no fear," agreed Jesus.

"No fear, no need for a weapon," said Lao Tzu.

"People laugh at this as a way to live," I said. "They see this as unsophisticated, childish, and weak."

Jesus looked sad. "They create their own hell."

"A baby is more powerful," said Lao Tzu. "It can cry all day and not be hoarse. It can grab your finger and not let go. How does it do this? It is in harmony with the Tao."

"Aiki," I said. "The martial arts tactic where the defender refuses to clash with the attacker. Instead, she blends with him—and uses that strength."

"Yes," said Jesus. "Spiritual power."

"Those who flow as life flows know they need no other force," said Lao Tzu.

"They feel no wear, they feel no tear, they need no mending, no repair," I said.

Lao Tzu looked at me with surprise. He turned to Jesus with his brows raised. "Did you hear what he just said?"

Jesus just grinned.

42
the kingdom of heaven

The Tao gave birth to One;

One gave birth to Two;

Two birthed Three;

Three birthed All things.

All things leave behind them the dark feminine force

from which they came.

They go forward to embrace the bright masculine force

into which they have emerged.

Breathing out emptiness,

feminine and masculine find harmony.

People hate loneliness and emptiness,

and yet leaders make use of these qualities.

So it is that some things

are increased by being diminished,

and being increased diminishes others.

What other people teach, I also teach.

The violent and strong do not die naturally or peacefully.

I will make this the basis of my teaching.

Suspended in infinite space, I gazed at the warm glow of Earth. My body hung in Dark Infinity, while my face was bathed in Earth Light.

And then I condensed into human form.

"They have names for that these days, you know," said Lao Tzu beside me.

"What's that?"

"Some call it an OBE, an out-of-body experience," he said.

As Jesus took a seat beside us, he said, "Others call it Cosmic Consciousness."

"What do you call it?" I asked.

"I call it the Kingdom of Heaven," said Jesus.

"I call it Reality," said Lao Tzu.

They looked at each other and smiled.

"Why don't others experience this?" I asked.

"Many do," said Jesus.

"Others fall into the illusion that they are inside their body," said Lao Tzu.

"Ugh!" I made a face. "They think they are meat walking."

"Or meat dreaming," said Lao Tzu.

"They are drunk," said Jesus. "One day they will sober up."

I couldn't help but laugh.

"What's so funny?" asked Lao Tzu.

"That the drunkest people on Earth think they are the most sober and sane," I said.

"They are the most dangerous," said Lao Tzu.

"Yes," said Jesus. "It makes me want to both laugh and cry."

"That reminds me, Jesus," I said. "Do you know the shortest verse in the Bible?"

He grinned. I knew he knew the answer, but I told him anyway: "Jesus wept."

43
the weak and the strong

The softest thing in the world

dashes against the hardest and overcomes it.

That which has no substance can enter

where there is no crevice.

From this I understand the strength of non-action.

Few can understand this wordless wisdom,

and the advantage that springs out of non-action.

Lao Tzu showed me a cup of water. "Which is the strongest?"
he asked. "The cup—or the water in the cup?"

"The cup," I said. "It is hard and holds the water."

He picked up a hammer. "Which will break if I hit it?"

"The cup," I said.

"Hard is always overcome by hard," he said. "While the
soft continues on its way."

That made me think of an old story. "The fox created a man of tar to catch a rabbit," I said. "The rabbit came along and said hello. The tar man said nothing. The rabbit kept talking—and ended up stuck to the tar man."

Lao Tzu shook his head. "He should have just kept on hopping down the bunny trail."

"Two thousand years ago my body was destroyed," Jesus said. "Today my spirit is as strong as it ever was."

"The body is dense spirit," said Lao Tzu. "The appearance dies, the essence continues."

We sat together silently.

44

the cosmic bug zapper

Fame or life—

which do you hold more dear?

Life or wealth—

which do you hold on to more tightly?

Keep life and lose everything else.

Keep everything else and lose your life.

Which will bring you sorrow?

Clearly, the person who pursues fame

loses that which is more valuable.

Those who want material riches,

give up true wealth.

If you are content with what you have,

you will not fear losing it.

If you know how to come to an end,

you will never be shamed.

You will live long, free from danger.

The three of us sat in Macy's Coffee House at a corner table. The place was buzzing with Northern Arizona exotic life forms.

"Everyone is headed toward the Cosmic Bug Zapper," said Lao Tzu.

I looked at Jesus, hoping for an explanation. He just smiled and shook his head. "Humor him."

"When you reach the Place of Zap," Lao Tzu continued, "only your essence will go through." He held up his hand, and a holographic vision of the Place of Zap hung in the air between us. On one side was a large assortment of Zapped bodies, back packs, autobiographies, and self-portraits of people kissing the backs of their own hands. On the other side were light beings with varying expressions on their faces: relief, amazement, pleasure, amusement, and shock. As I watched, the light beings continued journeying on their way, leaving everything behind.

"What's in the backpacks?" I asked.

"Those were the monkeys on their backs," said Lao Tzu.

"Attachments," said Jesus.

"They did not feel whole, so they looked to fill the hole," added Lao Tzu.

"With what?" I asked.

"With everything that will never fill it," said Jesus.

We watched as others approached the Cosmic Bug Zapper. Some went through with almost no zap sound at all.

"Their attachments and treasures were already on the other side," explained Jesus.

The Place of Zap disappeared. I looked around the coffee shop. I saw that many people looked as if they were carrying heavy burdens.

But others beamed with joy.

45

right here

When you pay little attention to your achievements,

your strength endures.

You find the greatest satisfaction

in that which looks like emptiness.

The ocean's tide is never exhausted.

The straight way seems crooked.

Your greatest skill seems clumsy,

and your eloquence a stammering scream.

Constant action overcomes cold;

being still overcomes heat.

Purity and stillness are the way to guide the world.

"Look at her," said Lao Tzu. "She's all sad because you didn't show up, Jesus. She wanted you to come with blazing light and sounding trumpets." He shook his head. "See the way her bottom lip is poked out? She's in a sulk."

"But I'm right here," said Jesus.

And then I heard Buddha say, "So am I."

And then Krishna said, "So am I."

"So am I," said Yahweh.

"So am I," said Allah.

"So am I," said Ganesha.

"So am I" said Moses.

"So am I," said God.

"So am I," said Muhammad.

"So am I," said Solstice Light.

All the many forms of the Source said one by one and in unison, "So am I."

"So am I," I said.

We formed a circle, and we laughed while we danced and sang.

46
fear

When the Tao prevails in the world,

tractors and farm machinery are the most useful vehicles.

When the Tao is disregarded,

war machines stand ready along the borders.

There is no guilt greater than to cherish your ambition;

no calamity greater than to be discontented with your lot;

no fault greater than the wish to accumulate things.

The sufficiency of contentment

is enduring and unchanging.

"Fear is a condom on the heart," said Lao Tzu.

"It thinks it's protection?" I asked.

Jesus shook his head. "All it's doing is preventing new birth."

"When the heart wears a condom over its head," asked Lao Tzu, "how can it see?"

"And since it can't see," said Jesus, "it wants to be armed with a weapon."

I imagined my heart inside a condom. "Partially blind and armed, it will fire at will," I said. "At anyone's will but its own."

Lao Tzu nodded. "But the heart without a condom of fear will not be angry."

"The naked heart is both male and female—and neither," said Jesus.

"All opposites collapse," I agreed.

Lao Tzu looked at me and put his hand over his mouth. "Oh no! That means we are each other!"

"Jesus," I whined, "he's messing with me again."

Jesus laughed.

And then, with hearts distinctly different, our hearts became the same.

47
dung beetle

You don't need to leave your home

to understand the world.

You don't need to look out the window

to see the Tao.

The farther you go away from yourself,

the less you know.

That's why the wisest people gain wisdom

while rooted in one place.

They correctly recognize a reality they have never seen.

They accomplish much without ever having any ambition.

The three of us were lying on our stomachs, watching a dung beetle roll its ball of shit.

Lao Tzu propped his chin in his hands. "What do you think it would say if we asked it, 'What is the meaning of life?'"

I kicked my heels in the air. "It would say the meaning of life is to get all this shit done."

Jesus snorted. "Poor beetle," he said. "It cannot see what we see. Nor can anyone in that frame of mind."

We rolled over and sat up. Lao Tzu looked at me. "What is worth seeing?" he asked.

I sat silently for a moment, opening, and then I said, "The essence of all being and its expansion."

"Not Disney World?" he asked.

I laughed and shook my head.

"Where is it to be found?" asked Jesus.

"To quote a dear friend," I told him, "the Kingdom of Heaven is within."

"The portal to the essence of all being is at your core," said Lao Tzu.

"That's what I said," said Jesus.

48
nekkid

If you devote yourself to learning,

you'll seek to increase your knowledge daily.

If you devote yourself to the Tao,

you'll seek daily to do less.

Each day, you'll do a little less and a little less,

until finally you will arrive at non-action.

Once you have achieved non-action,

there will be nothing you do not do.

If you want to own everything in the world,

you will do so by letting it all go.

If you do your best to hold on to everything in the world,

you will have nothing.

Lao Tzu asked Jesus, "Are you a Christian?"

Jesus replied, "Are you a Taoist?"

They laughed and then looked at me.

"I keep being reborn," I said.

Jesus nodded. "How are you doing with being flesh?"

"I remember when I was a meat head," said Lao Tzu.

"I appreciate my body," I said.

"To go through the next birth canal," Jesus warned, "you have to take off your clothes."

"Nekkid you came into this world," Lao Tzu said, "and nekkid you go out."

Jesus held up a finger. "That includes doctrinal clothes, too."

"Get shed of them," said Lao Tzu.

"I don't even know nothing," I said.

49
tschhh...

The wise person never makes up her mind for herself.

Instead, she is open to the ideas of others.

To those who are good to me, I am good—

and to those who are not good to me, I am also good.

And thus all receive goodness.

To those who are sincere, I am sincere—

and to those who are not sincere, I am also sincere.

And thus all receive sincerity.

The wise person appears to be indecisive.

He seems indifferent to everything.

People pay attention to what he does,

and he treats them all as lovingly

as if they were his children.

Early one morning, we sat together on the beach.

The gentle waves rolled in, rolled out.

Tschhh . . . tschhhh . . . tschhh . . .

A sea bird cried.

50
walking by the lake

People enter this world and live.

They enter the world again and die.

Three out of every ten people will give life to themselves,

while another three will give themselves death.

Another three in every ten want to live,

but their actions bring them toward death.

Why? Because they try so hard to hold on to life.

The wise individual, one out of ten,

manages life so skillfully that she travels unafraid,

naked and weaponless,

among wild and dangerous animals.

The rhinoceros finds no place in her

into which to thrust its horn,

the tiger cannot discover a place where it can fix its claws,

and no weapon can pierce any part of her.

Why? Because in her there is no place of death.

We were walking by the lake.

"I love you guys," I said.

Jesus gave me a smile. "We love you too."

"You are not always plotting and planning and scheming," I said.

"There is no place but here," said Lao Tzu.

"Here is no place for there," said Jesus.

Lao Tzu bumped Jesus with his shoulder. "Forgive me," said Lao Tzu.

"Can't do it." Jesus grinned. "I hold nothing against you."

Lao Tzu picked up a small rock and held it against Jesus' arm as we continued to walk.

After a while, Jesus asked Lao Tzu, "Tired yet?"

"Dang right!" Lao Tzu let the rock drop to the ground.

"Now you are forgiven," said Jesus.

We walked on, holding nothing against anyone.

51

circum-stance

The Tao gives birth to every creature in the universe.

Its outflowing nourishes everything.

Each thing receives its shape according to its nature.

Each becomes complete in harmony with its circumstances.

This is why the entire universe, without exception,

expresses the Tao.

All things reveal its creative stream.

This expression is completely natural,

a spontaneous tribute.

In this way, the Tao births all things,

nourishes them, brings them to their full growth,

cares for them lovingly, completes them, matures them,

maintains them, and overspreads them.

It births them and makes no claim.

It quietly and humbly carries them

through each step of their existence.

This is the mystery of the Tao.

Lao Tzu was reading out loud to me. "'Every creature in the universe,'" he repeated. "Did you catch that?"

I nodded. "*Every* being."

"Without exception. It all expresses the Tao."

"We are all sons and daughters," Jesus said. "We are all offspring of the Father."

"And the Mother," said Lao Tzu.

"And It," I said.

Lao Tzu went back to reading out loud. "'Each thing receives its shape according to its nature. Each becomes complete in harmony with its circumstances.'" He paused and looked up at me. "Did you hear that, boy. *Your* circumstances!"

"What about them?" I asked.

"You are the Tao taoing," he answered. "And then the stance you take to what is around you—your 'circum'—shapes you."

"If you are a limp noodle," Jesus put in, "you'll stay a limp noodle."

"If you take a self-righteous, angry stance," Lao Tzu continued, "you are a match asking to be struck."

"And in the end," Jesus hummed, "the stance you take is equal to the trance you make."

"I think he's getting it," said Lao Tzu. He went back to reading. "'The Tao births all things, nourishes them, brings them to their full growth, cares for them lovingly, completes them, matures them, maintains them, and overspreads them.'"

"I love It!" I said.

My stancing became dancing, and the three of us danced on down the road.

52
the light of awareness

The Tao that birthed each thing in the universe

is the Mother of all.

When you find the Mother,

you recognize her children.

When you know you are your Mother's child,

you guard Her qualities within you,

throughout your entire life.

Stop talking. Close the gateway of your heart.

Cease striving,

and your inner nature will remain safe.

But if you expend yourself, trying to get ahead,

you will lose your own identity.

If you are clear-sighted,

you will perceive even the smallest things.

If you are strong, you will guard

that which is soft and tender.

Use your light well.

Stay connected to its source.

And you will see eternity.

After we climbed the mountain, we rested for a while in a grove of aspen. "Close your eyes," said Lao Tzu.

I sat quietly with eyes closed.

"What do you see?" he asked.

"Light," I said. "Shining through my eyelids."

"Take your jacket," he said, "and put it over your head."

I put my jacket over my head.

"What do you see now?" he asked.

"I still see light."

"No movies of your mind?"

"No."

"You are seeing the past," he said. "The past which is present now. The light you are seeing is the light of the origin of all things."

"That light is you," said Jesus. "You are the light of the world."

"Do you also see the darkness?" asked Lao Tzu.

"Yes."

"That is Dark Energy from which all light arises," he said.

"You are like a tree," said Jesus. "Your roots are deep in the Ground of all existence. Your trunk and branches are in the Sky of being."

"Take that jacket off your head," said Lao Tzu.

I removed the jacket. The day was beautiful and bright.

We three trees got up and moved through the grove.

53
sounds familiar

If I were suddenly given a position

where I could govern others according to the Great Tao,

I would worry most that I might look as though

I was merely putting on a show.

The Great Tao's way is level and easy,

but people love to branch off on their own.

They spend their time decorating their houses,

and meanwhile the Earth is untended and barren.

They wear fancy clothes and carry powerful weapons.

They pamper themselves with food and drink.

They own far more than they need.

People like this are arrogant thieves.

They do not follow the Tao!

"Enough said," said Lao Tzu.

"The eye of the needle and all that," said Jesus.

"Some things just don't change," I said.

54

pebble in the pond

That which is planted by the Tao

can never be unrooted.

That which the Tao enfolds,

will never be destroyed.

Endless generations will honor

what has been accomplished.

If you nurture the Tao within you,

you will have both vigor and integrity .

Your family will be enriched.

Your community will thrive.

Your entire nation will prosper.

Observe how the Tao affects each level:

the individual, the family,

the community, the nation.

How do I know this is true?

By observation.

The surface of the pond was smooth.

"Drop a pebble in," said Jesus.

I did.

"What happened?"

"The pebble sank."

"Naturally," said Lao Tzu.

"What else?" asked Jesus.

"It made a splash," I said.

"That's fame, boy," said Lao Tzu. "Notice it and let it go."

"Something else happened," said Jesus. "Something is still happening."

I looked at the pond. "Ripples went out and are going out in all directions."

"That's what happened to us." Jesus pointed to himself and Lao Tzu.

"Still happening," said Lao Tzu.

"No end to it," said Jesus.

"Same with you." Lao Tzu jabbed my chest with his finger. "Virtue is a name for the energy of the Tao."

"Creative and transformative," said Jesus. "Healing."

"When you move in accord with the Tao," said Lao Tzu, "creative energy flows in all directions.

"How do I move in accord with the Tao?" I asked.

"Like this," said Jesus.

I looked at him. "You're not doing anything."

Lao Tzu laughed. "*Be!* That's all."

55

the direction of erection

If the Tao lives abundantly within you,

you are like a newborn baby.

Poisonous insects will not sting you;

fierce beasts will not attack you;

birds of prey will not swoop down on you.

The baby's bones are fragile and its muscles soft,

and yet its grasp is firm.

A baby boy knows nothing about sex,

and yet he can have an erection,

proving that his body is already complete.

He cries all day and never becomes hoarse,

proving the harmony of his being.

When you know this harmony,

you too will see the secret of eternity's way.

Life-giving wisdom will find you.

If you seek to save your life through your own skill,

you will find only evil.

If you try to control your life,

your strength will be false and empty.

Things that rely on their own strength

wear out and become old.

This is not the Tao's way.

Whatever does not follow the Tao

will come to an end.

We stood gazing into the inner basin of the dormant volcano, our backs to the vastness of the plains.

Lao Tzu shifted his weight from one foot to another. Clearly, he had something on his mind. "What?" I asked.

"You know how people get into trouble?" he asked.

"How?"

"They inflate themselves into an erection," he said.

The imagery made me laugh.

"Regardless of gender," said Jesus.

"Once inflated, they wander through life looking for satisfaction," said Lao Tzu.

"And they don't get no," I said. They looked at me with their eyebrows raised, so I sang a few bars of the Stones' song.

When I was done, Lao Tzu said, "It's like putting a head on top of your head."

"That bubble always bursts," said Jesus.

"Well, I guess we've got that figured out," said Lao Tzu.

"Your head is starting to show," said Jesus.

Lao Tzu laughed.

We turned and began our descent.

56

the postures of your mind

The person who truly knows the Tao

doesn't talk much about it;

the person who is always wanting to talk about the Tao

doesn't really know much about it.

If you know the Tao,

you will keep your mouth shut

and guard your senses.

You will round off your sharp edges

and unravel your complexities.

You will shield your own light

and be content to walk in others' shadows.

This is called the Mysterious Harmony.

Here you can be treated neither too familiarly

nor too distantly.

You are beyond all thought of either your own profit

or your own injury.

You are concerned with neither humility nor pride,

and yet you are equal to the person

with the highest position in the world.

"Cross your arms and legs," said Lao Tzu.

I did as I was told.

"How do you feel?" he asked.

I thought a moment and then answered, "Obstinate and secure."

"What else?"

"Defensive and protective."

"Now uncross your arms and legs," said Jesus.

I did as I was told.

"And now?" asked Lao Tzu. "How do you feel?"

"Now I feel open and aware."

"You are an open conduit," said Jesus.

"Instead of a knot head," said Lao Tzu.

"These are the postures of your mind," said Jesus.

"When you refuse the flow of the Tao," Lao Tzu said, "you become refuse."

Jesus laughed.

"When I resist the flow of Spirit, I re-cyst," I said.

They looked at me blankly.

"You know," I explained. "Become a cyst again."

Lao Tzu rolled his eyes. "Closed stance is a trance," he said.

"Open stance is a dance," said Jesus.

"I much prefer the open stance," I said.

"*Now* you are talking," said Lao Tzu.

57

an open meadow

A *peaceful country is governed directly,*

but wars use craftiness.

In the end, your realm is only your own

through selfless action and spontaneous purpose.

How do I know this is so? By these facts:

The more prohibitive laws a country has,

the poorer its people will be;

the more people worry about their own wealth,

the more disorderly the family and the country;

the more people plot and plan,

the more unnatural the land becomes;

and the more regulations and legislation are passed,

the more thieves and robbers there are.

Therefore, if you are wise, you will say,

"I will do nothing out of strife, to achieve my own ends—

and those around me will naturally

be transformed by themselves.

I will be fond of keeping still—

and let those around me figure out

their own correct paths.

I won't worry,

and my realm will spontaneously become rich.

I will let go of all ambition,

and my world will come into its natural simplicity."

Jesus, Lao Tzu, and I were walking across an open meadow, when all of a sudden, a fence encircled each of us. We were forced to stop where we were.

"Who are those people over there?" I asked, pointing.

"Interpreters of the meanings of the fences," said Lao Tzu.

"And those people over there?"

"Fence enforcers," said Jesus.

A third group was busy creating more fences.

"Here comes a fourth group," I said. "They look nasty and cunning."

"Fence violators," explained Lao Tzu.

"And this fifth group. Who are they?"

"They come to sell us weapons," said Jesus.

"Why do we need weapons?"

"To protect us from the violators," said Lao Tzu.

"And from each other," said Jesus.

"I thought we were getting along just fine," I said.

"We are," said Jesus.

"What do we do now?" I asked.

"Do you have a loving heart?" asked Lao Tzu.

"Of course," I said.

"Then just keep on walking."

The fences were gone, and the open meadow beckoned us once again.

58
the library

The government that is simplest,

is often best for the people.

When the government meddles with everything,

people become sneaky and dishonest.

In misery, happiness can be found,

and misery hides within happiness.

Who knows which will come out in the end?

So should we get rid of all government?

Good government is so easily distorted into evil.

People have been confused about this for a very long time.

Therefore, the wise person is like a square

with no hurtful sharp corners.

She is straightforward without hurting anyone,

and illuminated without any glare.

Jesus, Lao Tzu, and I were in the library looking at the magazines. Lao Tzu was scanning *Runner's World*, while Jesus was checking out *Scientific American*. I was reading *The Atlantic*.

I looked up at Jesus and asked softly, "What is the ultimate truth?"

Lao Tzu looked over to see what Jesus would say.

"Check out your body," whispered Jesus. "You have a right side and a left side."

I nodded.

"Your spine is in between, neither left nor right, yet both."

I nodded again.

Lao Tzu let his magazine drop into his lap. Clearly, he had decided our conversation was more interesting than whatever he had been reading.

"On what does your spine sit?" asked Jesus.

"This seat," I said.

"And what is beneath the seat?"

"The floor."

"And beneath the floor?"

"The Earth."

"And beneath the Earth?"

"Space."

"And beneath space?

"I don't know," I said.

"Exactly!" said Jesus.

Lao Tzu snorted. He tried to smother his laughter, but then he snorted again. His laughter was contagious. Jesus let out a whoop, and soon I was laughing so hard I had to wipe the tears from my eyes.

The librarian looked at us and shook her head. "You gentlemen will have to go outside."

We got to our feet and tiptoed out.

It was a lovely day.

59
light bulb

Moderation is the best way

to regulate your human desires

and serve Heaven.

Only through moderation

will you return quickly to your natural state.

I call that quick return the fullness of the Tao.

With the fullness of the Tao will come limitless freedom.

In this state, you will achieve control over your realm.

You will endure like a deeply rooted plant with a sturdy stalk.

This is the way to security and enduring life.

"Look at him," said Lao Tzu.

Jesus nodded. "He's a little aggravated."

"My body won't work right," I complained.

Lao Tzu raised his eyebrows and looked at Jesus. "I guess he hasn't let go."

Jesus turned to me. "Which is more important, the light bulb or the light?"

I sighed. I just wasn't in the mood for this nonsense. "They are both important, Jesus."

"Yep," Lao Tzu said, "he's in a dither."

"Foaming at the mouth," said Jesus.

"Will you stop it?" I sputtered. "Stop talking about me like I'm not here!"

"Light bulb or light?" asked Jesus.

I sighed again. "All right! Light!"

"Keep identifying with the light bulb," said Lao Tzu, "and you are headed for the landfill."

"What can we do to help you lighten up?" asked Jesus.

"Let's go wander around." I opened the door.

Outside, there was limitless freedom.

60
walking

Governing a great realm is like cooking small fish:

stir them and they break apart easily.

When the realm is governed according to the Tao,

the evil from the past loses its spiritual energy.

The energy is still there,

but it will no longer be used to hurt others.

It still has the power to be destructive,

but the ruler of the realm

has brought everything into unity and peace.

The ruler works in harmony with the past,

so that past and present converge for good

within the Tao.

As we walked together through the little downtown park, Lao Tzu turned to me and said, "Understand yourself and you understand the Cosmos."

Jesus nodded. "You are the Cosmos walking. Walking is a model of all relationship."

I pondered that a moment. "Because we slow down and see what's going on?"

Jesus smiled. "That and more."

"When you walk," asked Lao Tzu, "which goes first—your left leg or your right leg?"

"One keeps going after and before the other," I said. "There is no first or last."

"One of them had to make the first move," said Lao Tzu.

"Doesn't matter which one," I said. "As long as they accept each other's invitation to follow after."

"Notice that your breathing is in between the two," said Jesus, "and partial to neither."

"Your walking transports your breathing," said Lao Tzu.

I had to laugh at the thought of being breath walking.

"You are being breathed," Jesus reminded me. "You do not breathe yourself."

"The Tao, the Source is breathing you," said Lao Tzu.

We walked silently for a while through the park. Our

Source was breathing us, and we were taking our Source for a walk.

It was a beautiful day.

61
the trinity of self

A nation becomes great by being like a low-lying stream:

it becomes the center into which all the smaller streams flow.

Let me illustrate this from masculine-feminine interactions:

the feminine overcomes the masculine with her stillness.

You can think of stillness as a form of humility,

and yet by lowering yourself,

you gain everything.

In this way, great power yields to weaker,

and gains the smaller power for itself,

while small powers yield to greater,

and win favor.

The great power wishes only to unite and nourish others.

The smaller power wishes to serve and be protected.

Each gets what it wants.

But first the greater power must learn to be humble.

As we came out of the theater, the air was crisp and fresh. We had just seen *Lincoln*, and we were talking about the movie.

"A nation is like a self," said Lao Tzu. "The same principles apply."

"But what is a self?" I asked.

Lao Tzu put his hands in his pockets and walked a few more steps before he answered: "It's a mind made up."

Jesus nodded. "It tightens itself into a knot."

"I have trouble with my mind," I admitted.

Lao Tzu gave me sly sideways glance. "Who is the 'I' that has the trouble?"

I thought a bit. "My mind has trouble with the 'I.'"

Lao Tzu looked at Jesus. "He doesn't know who 'I' is."

Jesus looked at me. "Let not your mind be troubled," he said, "and you will know who 'I' is."

"When you know who 'I' is," said Lao Tzu, "then 'I' will disappear."

"No I, no self," said Jesus.

"That makes me scared," I said.

Lao Tzu laughed. "Now he has a 'me.'"

"Add a 'mine' and you have the trinity of self," Jesus said.

"You meet your self coming and going," said Lao Tzu.

"A hall of mirrors," said Jesus.

Lao Tzu slapped me on my back. "Wake up!"

I jumped and woke up. We were coming out the theater. We had just seen the movie *Lincoln*, and the air was crisp and fresh. . . .

62
the gateless gate

Tao is the heart of the universe.

It is the greatest treasure of those who are good,

and it guards even those who are bad,

counteracting their evil.

The Tao's words bring us honor.

Its deeds lift us up.

It never abandons anyone,

even those who are not good.

Better to be on your knees,

learning the Tao's lessons,

than to be the most powerful leader

surrounded by all the world's rank and riches.

Why did our ancient ancestors prize this Tao so much?

Wasn't it because those who seek it, find it?

And because in it, the guilty are forgiven?

This is why everything under heaven considers the Tao

to be the most valuable thing of all.

We had finished breakfast and were sitting around the table. I was lost in thought.

"Pay attention," said Lao Tzu. "Attend outside. What are you?"

"I am a particle in vast space," I said.

"Alone?"

I shook my head. "No. There's you, there's Jesus, there are all the other people, the animals, the plants, the Earth, galaxies, all the other beings, objects, and all the things in the world."

"Attend inside," said Jesus. "What are you?"

"I am vast space with thoughts, images, emotions, feelings, all forming and unforming.

"Which one is you?" asked Lao Tzu. "The vast inner space that is particularizing or the particle moving through vast outer space?"

I flickered back and forth.

"Stop!" said Jesus.

I did.

"Where did you stop?" he asked.

"Between the inside and the outside," I said.

"Which way are you looking?" he asked.

"Both ways," I said.

"That is the gateless gate," said Lao Tzu. "Infinity is in every direction, and its heart is everywhere."

I looked "down" and gasped. I had no body. I was the universe univers-ing.

A breakfast cup rattled. I solidified as George once again.

Jesus smiled. "Now you are ready to begin."

"You can start by doing those dishes, Mister Universe," said Lao Tzu.

We laughed and began clearing the table.

63
the Cosmos Gym

If you follow the Tao,

you will act without personal desire.

You will conduct your affairs

without concern as to the outcome.

You will taste everything

without caring about the flavor.

You will perceive small things as being great,

and few as important as many.

You will pay back injury with kindness.

You will plan ahead for what is difficult

with the ease of the present moment.

You will do great things one small step at a time.

Everything that's difficult now came into being

from a moment when they were still easy,

and all great things grew out of smallness.

That is why you will be able to accomplish great things

by doing only small things.

The person who makes a promise lightly

doesn't keep faith,

and the person who is always thinking things will be easy

is sure to find them difficult.

That is why the wise person sees difficulty

even in what seems easy,

and so he never has any problems getting things done.

Great things are accomplished with ease.

Lao Tzu said, "Let's go work out."

"Okay," said Jesus.

Lao Tzu looked me up and down. "You will need to change your close."

"You mean my clothes?" I asked him.

"Nope. Come on."

We arrived at the Cosmos Gym of Vast Space and No Effort and went in the door.

"Be still and know the I Am," said Jesus.

Immediately, I began flashing on scenes of my existing.

"Not the Me Am, you knucklehead," said Lao Tzu.

Me disappeared. The Cosmos was formed of space with intermittent tiny bubbles. All flowed with no effort, no effort at all, and great things were accomplished.

After no time, Lao Tzu said, "There is another room. Come with me."

Jesus and I followed him and peered through the doorway. Frowning people were lifting heavy weights. They looked worried and tired. Each worked out alone.

"What are those weights?" I asked.

"They have amassed the tiny bubbles into Duty and Responsibility," said Jesus. "It's hard work now."

"Do they know the other workout room exists?" I asked.

"Yup," said Lao Tzu. "But they think that's cheating."

"I told them my burden was Light," said Jesus, "but they don't listen."

"They love to eat their BST sandwiches," said Lao Tzu.

"You mean BLT," I said.

"Nope, BST," said Lao Tzu. "Blood, Sweat, and Tears."

"Enough?" Jesus asked us. We nodded and went out into the cool night air.

"Thanks for the workout," I said to Lao Tzu.

"No problem," he said.

64
Scrabble

When things are still,

they can be easily maintained.

It's easier to prevent something from happening

before it's given any indication of coming into existence.

That which is brittle is easily broken;

that which is very small can be easily scattered.

Action should be taken

before a thing has made its appearance;

order should be kept before disorder has begun.

A tree with a trunk as big as the circle of your arms

grew from the tiniest sprout.

The skyscraper started out as a small heap of stone.

The journey of a thousand miles

began with a single step.

The person who acts with ulterior motives does harm.

If she tries to grab something and make it her own,

it will slip from her grip.

If you're wise, you won't act like this.

You will not try to grasp anything selfishly,

and therefore nothing will fall from your hands.

People are constantly ruining their own affairs

when they are on the eve of success.

This wouldn't happen if they weren't trying

to force things to completion.

If you're wise,

you will desire what no one else wants.

You will place no value on things

that are difficult to achieve.

You will turn back and notice

what everyone else has passed by.

You will let all things take their course,

without any ulterior purpose of your own.

Jesus, Lao Tzu, and I were playing Scrabble. I put my letters down.

"That's not a word," Lao Tzu said.

"It is too."

Jesus just grinned.

"I-R-R-U-P-T, irrupt!" I said.

"It's spelled E-R-U-P-T, erupt, isn't it, Jesus?" Lao Tzu demanded.

"You can't lean on Jesus in this game," I said. "We follow the dictionary."

Lao Tzu scratched his nose. "If you are a word in the language of the Cosmos, what is your meaning?" he asked.

My mind went silent.

"And who is speaking you?" asked Jesus.

"The same One speaking you and Lao Tzu," I said.

"And your meaning?" asked Lao Tzu.

I'd had enough, at least for now, so I said, "To whip your butt at Scrabble."

Lao Tzu erupted with laughter and laughter irrupted into Lao Tzu. "Play the dang word," he said. "And let the game take its course."

65

mystic virtue

In the past, wise leaders who practiced the Tao

tried to make people simpler, not smarter.

People who are too clever are not easily led.

Rulers who depend on their own wisdom

damage their land,

while those who let go of their own knowledge

bless their realms.

When you understand these things,

you will apply them to your own life.

This is the mystic virtue,

which is deep and far reaching.

Those who follow it go against the world's grain,

while bringing all into a greater harmony.

On the other side of the meadow, Lao Tzu was lying on his belly looking at something.

"What is he doing over there?" I asked Jesus.

Jesus said, "Let's go see."

We found Lao Tzu staring at a little plant.

"What are you doing?" I asked.

"I'm giving this plant advice."

Jesus and I looked at each other and shook our heads.

I turned back to Lao Tzu. "What advice?"

"How to be a plant."

"But it already knows how."

"Well," he said, "I am further up the Emergence Chain than it is, so I know better."

"It gets all the advice it needs," Jesus said, "from its roots, from its opening to the sky."

"I thought I could help it be more clever," said Lao Tzu. "And get a jump on the other plants."

I snorted. "You want to jumpstart a plant?"

"Well, maybe it will work with you instead." He got up and stared into my eyes. "Do better! Get with it!"

I burst out laughing and whirled him around and 'round. We fell in a heap on the ground.

"Careful," said Jesus. "You are disturbing the plants."

apropos of nothing

We were in a store that sold secondhand clothes and other donations. I was looking at books, while Jesus was talking to the clerks, and Lao Tzu looked at children's toys.

"Look at this." He held up two wooden blocks. One had a 1 carved into it; the other a 0.

Jesus and I looked at the blocks.

"If you think you are 1, you are actually 0," Lao Tzu said.

My mind congealed. I looked at Jesus, hoping for direction.

Jesus said, "If you think you are something, you are nothing."

"There is no room in the In," said Lao Tzu.

Jesus laughed. "If you know you are 0, you are 1."

"Plenty of room then," said Lao Tzu.

"I see," I said. "If you know you are nothing, you are something."

"Yes," said Lao Tzu. "Here." He handed me the blocks. "Buy these. Tomorrow we will get into 2 and 3."

66
the people

The reason the great rivers and the sea

receive tribute from the valley streams

is that the rivers and the sea lie lower than the valleys,

and thus their humility gives them power.

So it is with the wise person.

If you wish to be lifted up above others,

humble yourself below them.

If you wish to lead them,

be willing to walk behind them.

In this way, even though you are above others,

they will not be burdened by your weight.

Though you lead them, they are not injured.

People will naturally and effortlessly lift you up.

If you do not strive against people,

no one will strive against you.

"Below, behind, above, and ahead," said Lao Tzu. "That's the wise person."

"I guess she has the people surrounded," I said.

"The people do not know whether she is coming or going," said Jesus.

"And neither does she," said Lao Tzu.

"Who do you think the people could be?" asked Jesus, looking at me.

"I have a feeling you want to tell me," I said.

Lao Tzu thumped my ear. "Don't get wise with Jesus."

Jesus laughed and touched my ear with one finger.

"It still hurts," I said.

"That's because you are pouting," said Jesus.

I laughed and the pain went away.

"The people could be all the voices and images inside you," said Jesus.

"The wise person allows them to rise and fall without engaging them," said Lao Tzu.

"They are happy because they think they are independent," said Jesus.

"Ah," I said, "and anything thinking it is independent has a short and isolated life span."

"You got it," said Lao Tzu.

"The wise person is detached," said Jesus. "He does not play the people's game."

I frowned. "I can't hear a thing you are saying."

Lao Tzu thumped my other ear.

I realized I was pouting again.

67
the three

All the world says that while my Tao is great,

it yet appears to be inferior to other systems of teaching.

Its very greatness is what makes it seem to be inferior.

If it were like any other system,

then its true smallness would have been revealed by now!

But I have three precious things I value and hold fast.

The first is gentleness, the second is simplicity,

and the third is humility.

With gentleness I can be bold;

with simplicity I can be generous;

shrinking from taking precedence over others,

I am married to honor.

Nowadays people give up gentleness

and are all for being bold;

they give up simplicity, and are all for being liberal;

they aren't willing to be humble

and seek only to be foremost.

All this ends in death.

Gentleness is sure to be victorious even in battle.

It firmly maintains its ground.

If you are kind and gentle,

Heaven will save you.

Your very gentleness will protect you.

Jesus, Lao Tzu, and I sat on a bench across from the gargoyle church. We liked the view.

A woman in bridal dress and a man in suit emerged from the church. Well-wishers surrounded them.

"Have you ever been married?" I asked Lao Tzu.

"No," he said. "Have you?"

I just rolled my eyes. I didn't want to go there, so I turned to Jesus.

"No need to ask him," said Lao Tzu. "He is married to everybody."

Jesus laughed. "Everything is married to everything."

"What about Nothing?" asked Lao Tzu.

"Nothing is single," said Jesus.

Lao Tzu laughed.

The couple got in a car and drove off. After hugs and clamor and waves of goodbye, the others departed. It was silent once again.

68

the power of non-contention

The person who follows the Tao does not use force.

She does not lose her temper.

She does not engage with her foes.

When she leads, she does so with humility.

We look at her and say,

"She never contends with others.

That is what makes her strong.

She persuades others

to use their own strength for harmony.

She lives in harmony with Heaven's light."

Jesus, Lao Tzu, and I were walking along one of Observatory Mesa's back trails.

"I want to tell you a story," said Lao Tzu.

Jesus and I waited, expectant and silent.

Finally, Lao Tzu said, "An obnoxious drunk was bothering many people in an inn. A martial artist sitting at a table began to be upset as well. The drunk was getting more boisterous, lurching around and bumping into people. The martial artist was about to jump him.

"At that moment, a calm but very clear voice said, 'Hey!' The drunk turned to look. It was a little old man with twinkling eyes.

"'Come here,' he said to the drunk. He patted the empty seat beside him. The drunk stumbled over and sat down. He was soon weeping and telling the old man his troubles. The old man gave him a handkerchief, and they talked as if they were old friends."

We walked silently for a while.

"You were the little old man?" I asked at last.

He laughed. "No. I was the drunk."

69

steam

A master of the art of war said,

"I would rather act defensively than take the offensive.

I would rather retire a foot than advance an inch."

This is called marshalling your ranks,

where there are no ranks.

It is baring your arms to fight,

where there are no arms to bare.

It is grasping the weapon,

where there is no weapon to grasp.

It is advancing against the enemy,

where there is no enemy.

There is nothing worse than entering conflict lightly.

In doing so, you lose the kindness that is so precious.

When weapons are finally lifted,

the one who deplores the situation conquers.

I was upset, and the cold, bleak winter day outside my window did not help. I felt misunderstood and attacked

"You are on the warpath," said Jesus behind me.

"It's not me," I said. "It's them."

Lao Tzu snorted. "Listen to yourself."

"It takes two to make a war," said Jesus.

"Well, I don't need them anyway!" I said.

"It's you that needs to disappear, not them," laughed Lao Tzu.

"Let's go for a walk," said Jesus. "I want to show you something."

We bundled up, left the house, and crunched through the snow.

"Here it is," said Jesus. A natural hot spring sent up wisps of steam. "Climb in, boys!"

We took off our clothes in the brisk air and eased into the water's heat.

"Ahhh!" moaned Lao Tzu. "Perfect!"

I could feel all tension letting go, releasing as if it never existed.

"I think he is learning his lesson," said Lao Tzu to Jesus.

"What is that?" I asked.

"Be like water," said Lao Tzu.

I splashed water in his face. "I hate it when you quote Bruce Lee."

Jesus made a water cannon with his hands. He hit both me and Lao Tzu full in the face with a stream of water.

"Hey, Prince of Peace!" I sputtered. "Cool it!"

And then we all three hooted like the old friends we are.

70

at the Kickstand Cafe

My words are very easy to know

and very easy to practice;

and yet the world neither knows nor practices them.

My words have a basic and essential truth.

My deeds have authority.

But the world does not recognize them.

They who know me are few,

but that only makes me more precious.

The wise person may wear rough clothing,

but he carries a jewel in his heart.

Jesus, Lao Tzu, and I were at the Kickstand Cafe. The place was pleasantly busy, but we had a table to ourselves.

"What's it like being you?" Lao Tzu asked Jesus.

Jesus shrugged. "They built a church on top of me."

"Ouch!" said Lao Tzu.

"What's it like being you?" Jesus asked Lao Tzu.

"Invisibility," said Lao Tzu. "Only small children and people with childlike hearts notice my existence."

Jesus took a sip of his coffee. "Pretty much the same for me."

They looked at me.

"What's it like being me?"

They nodded.

I thought a moment. "Happiness emerging, continuously emerging from the Wellspring."

They smiled. "Pretty much the same for me," they said in unison.

We sipped our drinks in silence.

71
sick of our sickness

To know and yet think you do not know is wisdom.

To not know and yet think you do know is sickness.

Flinch away from this disease,

and you will avoid it.

The wise person knows the pain that goes with this sickness,

and therefore she does not catch it.

Jesus and I were walking down the street. "Where is Lao Tzu?" I asked.

Just then we heard a strangely repetitious sound approaching. *Bam!* . . . *Bam!* . . . *Bam!* Lao Tzu was jumping up and down, up and down, on a pogo stick. He jumped 'round and 'round us.

"I have a question for you," he said as he bounced.

"What?" I asked.

"How many times must one jump on a pogo stick?"

My thoughts stuttered, stopped, but Jesus burst out with laughter. He asked, "How many times must one swear allegiance to the same set of thoughts?"

"Exactly!" said Lao Tzu and handed me the pogo stick.

I hid behind Jesus. "Don't give me that thing!"

Lao Tzu threw the stick high into the air where it disappeared.

"I feel better already," he said.

72

When you don't fear what you ought to fear,

what you fear the most will come to you.

Don't indulge yourself thoughtlessly in your ordinary life.

Don't act as though you're bored by life itself.

Avoid indulgence, and you will also avoid boredom.

If you're wise, you'll understand yourself

without parading your knowledge in front of others.

You'll love yourself without being conceited.

You'll stop worrying about what others think

and focus on the inner life.

On a summer day, we lay on our backs in the meadow. Soft white clouds floated above us in the blue, blue sky.

"All the people you know," said Lao Tzu, "are within you."

"No," I said. "They are out there." I waved my arm over my head.

Lao Tzu shook his head. "They are voices in your head and images in your heart."

"They are like clouds floating in the sky of your consciousness," said Jesus.

We fell silent. The wind blew through the trees.

I still wasn't convinced. "I can take you to them, at least some of them."

"You can make the meat meet the meat," said Lao Tzu. "Yet even then they are as you imagine them."

I frowned at the clouds. "What about if I set myself aside, and really, really listen, listen deeply?"

"Now you're talking," he said.

"They are definitely not separate from you then," said Jesus.

"Everything you imagine, sense, see, feel is you," said Lao Tzu.

"That's what loving your neighbor as yourself means," said Jesus. "It is opening to this awareness."

My heart smiled with the vastness of its being.

A bird sang a single note.

73

vast is Heaven's net

When your courage is reckless, you lose your life.

When your courage is cautious, you'll live.

When it comes to these two kinds of courage,

one is destructive, and the other is constructive.

But when Heaven smites you,

you never know for sure the reason.

Even the wise person doesn't understand fate.

Heaven moves without strife,

and yet it overcomes all.

It is silent, and yet it evokes a reply.

It never calls, and yet we come to it naturally.

It reveals itself quietly, yet with great power.

Heaven's net is vast.

Its mesh is large, and yet nothing escapes it.

As we sat in the park, a woman ran by trying to catch her dog. The dog appeared to be fleeing for its life.

"If you want something to come near you," mused Lao Tzu, "do not chase it."

I nodded. "Instead, create a vacuum."

The woman stopped running and began walking back our way. The dog also stopped running. It meandered around, nose to ground.

"Good morning," said Jesus to the woman.

"Good morning," she said. "I can't catch my dog."

Jesus laughed. "I've had the same trouble with sheep."

"Are you a shepherd?" she asked.

He shrugged. "Some say so."

"Judging by the company he keeps," said Lao Tzu, "I'd say he is more of a goat herder."

I laughed. "Are you saying you and I are a couple of old goats?"

The dog ran up to Lao Tzu and licked his hand.

"Well, I'll be darned," said the woman.

"Vast is Heaven's net," said Lao Tzu, "and nothing can slip through it."

"I like that," said the woman. "Who said that?"

"I did," he said.

She went on her way. The dog followed at her heels.

74

set up

When people have no fear of death,

there's no point in threatening them with death.

If death is people's worst fear, however,

then there will always be an executioner.

Even then, though,

there is always One who presides over death.

If you try to take that One's place,

you are like a person who hacks at wood

instead of letting the master carpenter do the building.

You'll just end up cutting your own hands!

Lao Tzu, Jesus, and I were at the Internet Café. Jesus sat looking around him with open and calm awareness. Lao Tzu was staring into his coffee cup as if the future of humankind was written there. I was surfing the web for the morning news.

"Listen to this," I said. "A man in Australia, on the hot summer day yesterday, waded into a shallow small pond. A large crocodile had also taken refuge there. The crocodile grabbed him and ate him. His friends said since boyhood he had been continuously fearful and wary of being eaten by a crocodile."

Jesus' eyes grew sad.

"He was devoured by his worst fear," said Lao Tzu.

"As we always are," said Jesus.

75
the dance of life

People starve when they're taxed too heavily.

People rebel when their leaders are self-seeking.

People don't worry about dying

when they are focused on living.

Don't focus all your energies on your goals,

and life's true meaning will reveal itself.

We sat on a bench across the street from the Church of the Nativity, the one where in winter the likeness of Jesus sometimes wore a snowball on its head. The San Francisco Peaks were visible in the distance.

Jesus was reading aloud from Lao Tzu's chapter 75. When he was done, he looked at Lao Tzu and nodded.

I said, "It is the same now as it was in Lao Tzu's time."

Jesus said, "It is easier for a camel to go through the eye of a needle than for a rich person to enter the Kingdom of Heaven."

"Why is that so?" I asked.

"Attachment," said Lao Tzu. "Attachment to what does not matter."

Jesus sighed. "Which is the same as saying: attachment to matter."

"Ah!" I said. "Thinking that only matter matters."

They looked at me.

"Your jest speaks more wisdom than you know," said Lao Tzu. "The life force is what is mattering. It is what is continuously emerging."

"Yes," said Jesus. "Matter does not matter. Only Spirit matters. Matter is the condensing, the solidifying of Spirit."

"Matter is Spirit dancing," said Lao Tzu.

I got up and began to make some moves. "You mean like this?"

"No." Lao Tzu hopped to his feet. "More like this!"

"And this!" said Jesus, moving with rhythmic flow.

The three of us danced and danced, and my heart focused on nothing but laughter.

76
the big cake in the sky

A newborn's body is supple and soft.

By the time he grows old and dies,

he has become hard and rigid.

So it is with all things.

Trees and plants, in their early growth,

are soft and flexible;

at their death, dry and withered.

See! Hardness and strength go along with death,

but softness and weakness

have life as their companion.

That is why you won't conquer

if you rely on your own strength.

The largest trees are cut down for use.

Strength is inferior,

while weakness is superior.

Birds were singing in the trees as we walked through the cemetery. The world around me was filled with light and sound, but I was intensely aware of the human remains beneath the ground.

"What happens when you die?" I asked.

"Separation," said Jesus and Lao Tzu simultaneously. Then they looked at each other and grinned.

"I know that," I said. "That is why we who are left behind grieve. We're separated from the ones we love."

"That is not what we mean," said Jesus.

Lao Tzu shook his head. "Nope. Think instead—what happens to an egg you crack to bake a cake?"

"The yolk and white go in the cake, and the shell goes in the compost pile."

"Same with death," said Lao Tzu.

I stopped walking and scratched my chin. I was confused.

"The soft and supple spirit separates from the hard and rigid body," explained Jesus.

"The body goes in the compost pile," said Lao Tzu.

"Where does the spirit go?" I asked.

"To quote Lao Tzu, it has 'life as its companion,'" said Jesus.

"Which is where it has always been," said Lao Tzu.

I continued walking again. "Though the egg often thinks it is just a shell game."

Lao Tzu groaned and gave me a gentle shove. "Be careful, boy, or we will send you to that Big Cake in the Sky."

"Sounds mighty fine to me," I said.

We left the cemetery and continued our stroll.

77

pulling down the high

and lifting up the low

Heaven's way is like bending a bow.

The part of the bow that was long is shortened,

and what was short is stretched long.

So Heaven diminishes where there is superabundance

and fortifies where there is deficiency.

This is not the practice of human beings.

Instead, they take away from those who have not enough

to add to their own superabundance.

But the person who follows the Tao

takes from her own superabundance and gives to everyone.

She acts without claiming the results as her own.

She achieves without arrogance.

She is humble,

with no desire to flaunt her skills.

As I sat at my computer, staring into unseen space, Jesus and Lao Tzu walked into my room.

"What's up?" asked Lao Tzu.

Jesus smiled because he already knew.

"I have writer's block," I said. "Nothing is coming."

"You are not blocked," said Lao Tzu. "Nothing is what you are receiving."

I rolled my eyes.

"He speaks the truth," said Jesus. "When nothing comes, you need to stop at nothing."

"What?" I was thoroughly confused.

"Stop at nothing, at no-thing, at not-hinged," Jesus said. "You need to become unhinged."

"And how do I do that?"

Lao Tzu tapped me on the head. "Release!"

"*Solvitur ambulando*," said Jesus. "It is solved by walking. Release comes from walking around. So let's go. Get up."

I didn't move. "Where are we going?"

"Wide open spaces!"

"But I have a blog to write!" I protested. "People are expecting it."

They grabbed me under the arms and hauled me out the door.

"I feel better already," I said. "Let me go back in. Just for a minute."

They laughed and kept a firm hold on my arms.

"You take the cake," said Lao Tzu.

We headed north toward the mountains.

78

put it into practice

There is nothing in the world softer and weaker than water,

but nothing is better at wearing down what is hard and inflexible.

Nothing is more effectual than water.

Everyone knows that the soft overcomes the hard,

and the weak the strong,

and yet few put this knowledge into practice.

Therefore, a wise person said,

"The person who accepts his nation's shame

becomes its greatest honor,

and the person willing to bear others' pain

will become the world's ruler."

The truth is often a paradox!

We were sitting in lawn chairs beneath the blazing stars, while all around us crickets and cicadas throbbed their rhythms. I was thinking of the condition of the human world and its impact on the Earth.

"What do people really want?" I asked.

For a few moments my only answer was the creak and scratch of the crickets and the cicadas.

"Security," said Lao Tzu finally. "People want to feel secure."

"Love and understanding," said Jesus. "To love and be loved. To understand and be understood."

The silence claimed us once more. A gentle wind blew through the pines and ceased.

I sighed. "We cannot feel secure in our bodies. They go the way of the wind."

"Jesus has it right," said Lao Tzu. "We are secure when we are loving, when we are understanding."

"When we love, we move beyond our self-admiration and self-hatred," said Jesus.

"When we love we have no need for security," said Lao Tzu. "We are larger than ourselves."

The crickets and cicadas went silent for a moment, then started up again.

"I thought you guys were supposed to be funny," I said.

"Ask your question again," said Lao Tzu.

"What do people really want?"

"To be entertained." Lao Tzu raised his hand and squirted me in the face with a water pistol.

"Hey!" I sputtered. "What did you do that for?"

"I was just trying to dissolve the hard and inflexible."

Jesus laughed. We got up and went inside, while the crickets and cicadas continued their endless song.

79
demanding nothing

When a long argument has finally been reconciled,

the one who was in the wrong

will often continue to nurse a grudge.

This is not good for either party,

neither the one in the wrong nor the one in the right.

To prevent this, don't keep a tally of wrongs,

and don't insist on being quickly paid back after a slight.

If you follow the Tao,

you'll look at the situation objectively

rather than from your own selfish perspective.

Heaven's way shows no partiality or favoritism.

It is always on the side of good.

We walked downtown and sat on a bench in the square. The day was lovely, filled with warmth and sunshine. Gradually, I became aware that a man in the square was shouting about Jesus.

"Come to Jesus!" he bellowed.

I wanted to tell him that Jesus was right here. "Some of your followers really turn me off with their aggressiveness," I said to Jesus.

"Look at it from their perspective," said Lao Tzu. "They think they are saving your soul from hell."

"Well, I wish they would lighten up."

Jesus smiled at me. "That's it exactly. Become the Light that lights the world."

I lightened up—and found that I did not mind the man's shouting so much.

We sat quietly and watched a couple of little kids zooming around on tricycles. Meanwhile, the man was still shouting.

I watched him for a while. "He is the one in hell," I observed. "His soul is writhing in anguish."

"I'll go speak with him," said Jesus.

He got up and went to the man. The man's yelling stopped.

Lao Tzu and I silently watched the white clouds floating in the deep blue sky while we waited for Jesus to come back. After a few minutes, he sat down again beside me.

"What did he say?" I asked.

Jesus gave me a rueful smile. "He wanted me to accept Jesus."

"What did you say?" asked Lao Tzu.

"I said I already knew him. He got pretty happy."

"Well, we have something in common with that fellow after all," said Lao Tzu.

"What's that?" I asked.

"We're both happy that we know Jesus too," said Lao Tzu.

"And I'm happy I know you two," said Jesus.

We got up and headed for the little pond. We were hoping to see the eagle, the heron, and the osprey.

80
lullaby

The best nation is a small one with few people.

Although they have abundant skills,

no one needs to rely on them.

No one seeks death,

but no one avoids it either.

They have vehicles

but no reason to ride in them.

They have armor and weapons

but no occasion to use them.

The people go back to older, simpler ways

of communicating.

They consider plain food to be the best,

and they prefer simple clothing.

They like ordinary pleasures.

They hear the sounds and voices

from the neighboring land,

but they would never travel there,

because they are content with their own land.

I was sitting in my living room contemplating the consciousness state of humankind when Jesus and Lao Tzu came in.

"Come with us," said Jesus.

I got up. Jesus took my right hand, Lao Tzu my left. Within an instant, we were in outer space, looking at the Earth.

"I can't breathe," I gasped.

"Yes, you can," said Jesus.

He was right. I looked "down" and saw I had no body.

"Your body is the entire universe," said Jesus.

"We are an interflow with all that is," said Lao Tzu.

The golden glowing Earth sang a soft song.

"What is the Earth singing?" I asked.

"A lullaby to its human offspring," said Lao Tzu. "Listen."

Gradually, I could understand the Earth's words:

O my children, settle down, settle down,

with your roots in the ground.

O my children, rise up, rise up.

your hearts opening to the sky.

I was filled with calm and peaceful energy.

The next instant, we three were standing together on the grass of the little downtown park.

"Rooting in the ground, opening to the sky," said Lao Tzu.

I understood. We began moving in rhythmic Tai Chi flow, rooting in the ground, opening to the sky.

I felt the Earth smile.

81

spiritual math

Sincerity doesn't worry about being pleasant.

Pleasant words aren't necessarily sincere.

Those who follow the Tao most closely

don't get in arguments about the Tao.

People who love to argue aren't familiar with the Tao.

Those who know the Tao don't flaunt their knowledge.

Those who need everyone to recognize their wisdom

don't know the Tao.

The wise person doesn't accumulate things for herself.

The more she helps others,

the richer she becomes;

and the more she gives to others,

the more she possesses.

Heaven's way is keen-edged,

but it never injures.

The wise person accomplishes much,

but he never strives.

Jesus, Lao Tzu, and I strolled over to the university. I looked around the empty campus. "Where is everybody?"

"Spring break," said Lao Tzu. "They have been released."

We walked into an empty classroom and sat down. After a moment, Jesus got up and walked over to the large board at the front of the room. "Time for a spiritual math lesson."

He wrote 1 + 1 on the board.

"What do you think of that?" he asked.

"Well, now you've got two," said Lao Tzu.

Jesus nodded. "That's this world—the world of duality, the horizontal world of linear time."

His words reminded me of something. "My grandfather once asked me: 'When you have to and you don't want to, what do you do?'"

They looked at me with their eyebrows raised.

"You give one away," I said.

Jesus smiled, and then he wrote 1 x 1 on the board.

"Ah!" Lao Tzu tilted his head back and spread wide his arms. "That's it!"

I frowned. "What's it?"

Jesus pointed at me. "What is 1 x 1?"

"1." I was still confused.

"Spiritual math," said Jesus. "If you are looking for God, the Wellspring, the Source, the Origin, you do not add yourself. You merge."

"1 x 1 is the spiritual path," said Lao Tzu.

"It is not out here," said Jesus. He erased the board. "It is within you."

We left the building, arm in arm, a strong and gentle force, merging, on the move.

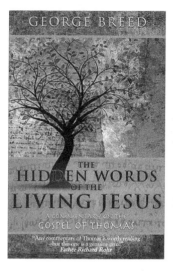

**The Hidden Words
of the Living Jesus:
A Commentary on
the Gospel of Thomas**
Author: George Breed
Price: $19.99
Paperback
Ebook Available
272 pages
ISBN: 978-1-937211-88-2

With his trademark earthy exuberance, author George Breed explores the deep meanings within the Gospel of Thomas, giving readers new and surprising insights into the message of Jesus.

"The Gospel of Thomas is emerging as a true mystical source from the earliest period of what became Christianity. Any commentary on Thomas is worth reading—but this one is a genuine gem!"
—**Fr. Richard Rohr, O.F.M.**, Center for Action and Contemplation, Albuquerque, New Mexico

"In this lovely book, Dr. George Breed helps to advance the art of seeing, not what rests on surfaces but rather that which lies through and beyond exteriors and forms, and within ourselves."
—**Bradley Olson, Ph.D.**, Jungian Depth Psychologist

**Brother Lawrence:
A Christian Zen Master**
Author: Anamchara Books
Price: $12.95
Paperback
Ebook Available
104 pages
ISBN: 978-1-933630-97-7

The winter I was eighteen, I stood looking at the bare branches of a tree. . . . My awareness was suddenly opened, so that I saw God.

This is the beginning of Brother Lawrence's spiritual journey, a journey that made him stand out to the Christian community of his day (he lived c. 1614-1691), not because he was a great thinker, a gifted speaker, or a talented writer–but simply because of the way he lived his life.

This way of life echoes the teachings of Zen. Surrender yourself to God and you will be equally at peace in both suffering and joy, Brother Lawrence told one of his visitors. When a person does not cling, wrote the Buddha centuries earlier, she is not agitated.

Song of a Christian Sufi:
A Spiritual Memoir
Author: Marietta Bahri Della Penna
Price: $24.95
Paperback
Ebook Available
ISBN: 978-1-937211-76-9

If Sufism acknowledges one central truth it is that we are not separate from the Divine, nor have we ever been. And yet at the same time, we know that the Beloved is always the initiator: God loves us long before we love God. The Divine is pursuing us before we ever think to pursue God. But we can recognize this only by unveiling our inner eye, that is, the eye of the heart.
—Song of a Christian Sufi

This is this the story of a woman's spiritual journey: from the restrictions of growing up as Catholic female in the 1950s to her emotional and spiritual liberation as a Sufi—and to her ultimate return to a deeper and richer Christianity. Sometimes funny, sometimes heartbreaking, her story resonates with anyone seeking to find life's deeper meanings. Della Penna's discovery of her own unique "song" is a gift to us all!

Anamchara Books
Books to Inspire
Your Spiritual Journey

In Celtic Christianity, an *anamchara* is a soul friend, a companion and mentor (often across the miles and the years) on the spiritual journey. Soul friendship entails a commitment to both accept and challenge, to reach across all divisions in a search for the wisdom and truth at the heart of our lives.

At Anamchara Books, we are committed to creating a community of soul friends by publishing books that lead us into deeper relationships with God, the Earth, and each other. These books connect us with the great mystics of the past, as well as with more modern spiritual thinkers. They are designed to build bridges, shaping an inclusive spirituality where we all can grow.

To find out more about Anamchara Books and order our books, visit **www.AnamcharaBooks.com** today.

Anamchara Books
Vestal, New York 13850
www.AnamcharaBooks.com

Made in the USA
Las Vegas, NV
02 January 2025

15742149R00142